The boundaries of
modern Iran

The SOAS/GRC Geopolitics Series

Territorial foundations of the Gulf states
EDITED BY Richard Schofield

The boundaries of modern Iran
EDITED BY Keith McLachlan

The Horn of Africa
EDITED BY Charles Gurdon

The boundaries of
modern Iran

EDITED BY

Keith McLachlan

Geopolitics and International Boundaries Research Centre
School of Oriental and African Studies
University of London

St. Martin's Press
New York

First published in 1994 by UCL Press.

The name of University College London (UCL) is a registered
trade mark used by UCL Press with the consent of the owner.

First published in the United States of America in 1994

Printed in Great Britain.

ISBN: 0-312-12062-1

Library of Congress Cataloging-in-Publication Data

The boundaries of modern Iran / edited by Keith McLachlan.
      p.   cm. — (The SOAS/GRC geopolitics series)
   Includes index.
   ISBN 0-312-12062-1
   1. Iran—Boundaries.   I. McLachlan, K. S. (Keith Stanley)
II. Series.
DS254.8.B68 1994
911'.55—dc20   93-40359
                                                CIP

Typeset in Palatino.
Printed and bound by
Biddles Ltd, King's Lynn and Guildford, England.

Contents

v

Preface

This volume reviews the key issues affecting Iranian boundaries and offers an analysis of the evolution of the country's frontiers over the historic period. In all, its constituent chapters make up a detailed summary of the emergence of Iranian boundaries and state territory and the tensions that still affect them. Each of Iran's borders with its principal neighbours is discussed in separate chapters. Abbas Maleki, Deputy Minister in the Iranian Ministry of Foreign Affairs, examines the northern frontier zone from an Iranian standpoint in Chapter 2, a study complementary to Professor Ganji's overview of key events affecting the boundary situation in Azerbaijan in Chapter 4. Keith McLachlan deals with the changes in the ownership of territory during the Iran–Iraq war of 1980–88. The origins of dispute over the Shatt al-Arab border are reviewed by Richard Schofield in Chapter 8. In addition, three authors offer illuminating explanations of matters directly touching on border problems – Richard Tapper analyzes the implications of Shahseven tribal politics on the international borders of northwest Iran in Chapter 3, Maria O'Shea, a specialist on Kurdish affairs, looks at the inter-relationship between notions of a Kurdish entity and the establishment of international boundaries in Chapter 5, while Bruce Ingham debates the linkages between language, ethnicity and local frontiers in southwest Iran in Chapter 7. Pirouz Mojtahed-Zadeh looks at the development of Iranian borders in the southeast (Ch. 10) and also dissects problems affecting the ownership of the disputed Persian Gulf island of Abu Musa in Chapter 9.

These various studies demonstrate that Iran's borders with its neighbours have been ever-fluctuating in recent centuries and that the hurried frontier delimitations of the late 19th and early 20th centuries have left a legacy of problems, not all responsive to immediate solutions. At a time of great uncertainty in the wake of the end of the Cold War, the uneven strides made towards instituting a new international order and Iran's search for identity as a post-revolutionary nation-state, security for the Iranian state is more closely than ever bound up with confidence in firm and settled frontiers. This book suggests, however, that Iran will not easily escape its difficulties and that tensions will persist in respect of profoundly complex boundaries such as those along the Shatt al-Arab and on the continental shelf of the Persian Gulf.

The opinions expressed in this volume are those of the authors. Maps showing international boundaries are for illustration only and should not be regarded as authoritative.

Acknowledgements are due to a number of people. The Geopolitics and International Boundaries Research Centre is indebted to the Institute for Political and International Studies in Tehran and the Department of Geography at the University of Tehran for their co-operation in staging the original seminar that inspired this publication, held at SOAS in December 1991. I thank Patricia Toye and Liz Paton for their copy-editing and Catherine Lawrence for her cartography. Thanks also go to Roger Jones and Nick Esson of UCL Press for publishing this collection.

It should be noted that transliteration in this book has, wherever possible, been made internally consistent and has been simplified. However, authors have been given discretion to employ the system of transliteration of their choice where they have felt strongly about the English language spelling of particular place names and real names.

Contributors

Muhammad Hassan Ganji Professor of Geography, University of Tehran.

Bruce Ingham Senior Lecturer in Linguistics, School of Oriental and African Studies, University of London.

Abbas Maleki Deputy Minister in the Iranian Ministry of Foreign Affairs.

Keith McLachlan Director, Geopolitics and International Boundaries Research Centre, School of Oriental and African Studies, University of London.

Pirouz Mojtahed-Zadeh Research Associate, Geopolitics and International Boundaries Research Centre, School of Oriental and African Studies, University of London.

Maria O'Shea Research Associate, Geopolitics and International Boundaries Research Centre, School of Oriental and African Studies, University of London.

Richard Schofield Deputy Director, Geopolitics and International Boundaries Research Centre, School of Oriental and African Studies, University of London.

Richard Tapper Reader in Anthropology, School of Oriental and African Studies, University of London.

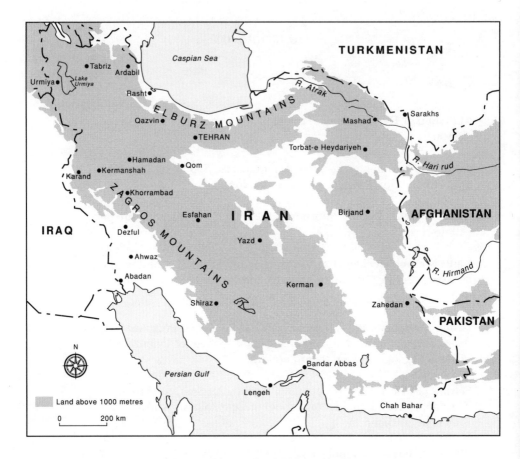

Figure 1.1 Iran and neighbouring states.

CHAPTER ONE
Introduction

Keith McLachlan

Traditional regions and national frontiers

Iran has functioned for at least 5,000 years as a state and the centre of an empire. During this considerable period its boundaries with its neighbours have been relatively fluid (Fig. 1.1).[1] Nonetheless, despite the powerful influences working against the need for hard and fast borders, of which Islam is perhaps the principal one, contemporary Iran under both the Pahlavi regime and the Islamic republic has adopted very clear policies towards defining and protecting state territory.

The administration of Iran has historically been plagued with difficulties of exerting authority outside the main areas of population and, therefore, in fixing its national frontiers. Iran is a vast and diverse country of 1,648,000 km², only a tenth of which is under settled forms of economic use. The rest is desert, steppe and high mountain. In many ways Iran was until the early 20th century a set of diverse ethnic and linguistic groups unified under a single government and sharing a common literature, social ethos and culture. The largest single provincial region by population size was Azerbaijan, where there was a concentration of Azhari speakers of the Turkic group of languages. Other coherent areas with a regional consciousness could be defined, including Kurdistan in the west, the Arab zone of the Khuzistan lowlands in the southwest, the Turkmen steppe of the north and the Baluch area of the southeast.

The Iranian territorial inheritance from the Qajar dynasty in 1921 was much reduced from earlier periods and weakly defined in international practice. This volume attempts to examine the evolution of the country's international boundaries in the contemporary epoch during which Iran has been buffeted by an apparently unending series of international and internal crises.

The territorial consolidation under Riza Shah

Riza Khan's and Sayyid Zia al-Din Tabatabai's *coup d'état* against the Qajars in February 1921 gave Iran a short breathing space of strong central control during which the idea of a modern nation-state was imposed on the country and the national borders made generally secure. This experience was important for Iran because it enabled the government to tie its many varied provinces firmly to the centre. Beginning in 1921, Riza Khan put down regional revolts by the tribes of the Khamseh and others before beginning the process of reducing rebellion elsewhere in the west.[2] Riza Khan took advantage of the Russian withdrawal from Iranian soil in September 1921 to put down the revolt of Kuchik Khan in the northern province of Gilan, marking the clear beginning of the centralization process. In the following year Riza Khan attacked rebel forces in Azerbaijan and Kurdistan and settled the northeast province of Khorasan. The process continued in 1923 in the south where the main tribes, the Bakhtiari and Qashqai, were put down and Shaikh Khazal, the regional ruler of Khuzistan, removed to Tehran.

The military consolidation of the power of the centre was developed in parallel with Riza Khan's seizure and legitimization of his own position. In 1925 Riza Shah began the political process of sealing the unity of the nation[3] by deposing the last of the Qajar dynasty, Muhammad Ali Shah, and setting in its place the House of Pahlavi.

Riza Shah's carefully constructed state and its national frontiers were, however, far from strong. The illusion of dominance from the centre worked only in relation to the internal provinces of the country. Iran's abilities to confront the outside world were very limited despite the building of the Iranian army. The Iranian authorities also successfully engaged in legal battles with the British in the form of the Anglo–Iranian Oil Company in the south and made some gains in the 1933 oil agreement.[4]

In 1941, what appeared to be a pro-German revolt by Rashid Ali in Iraq brought the Middle East region directly into the lines of conflict of the Second World War. Iran was declared neutral in this war but the Rashid Ali affair in Iraq and growing British suspicions concerning the activities of German agents in Iran put Iran's neutrality in jeopardy. The invasion of the USSR by German forces in June 1941 added to Iran's difficulties, since the Anglo–Soviet alliance exposed the country to simultaneous pressures from the north and the south. Iran increasingly became perceived by the allies as a strategic supply corridor for transferring war materiel to aid Russian defence.[5] Iran's oil was seen as a key commodity for the use of the allies, also to be denied the axis powers.[6] Iran was occupied by the British and Russians on 25 August 1941.

The challenge of the autonomous republics in the 1940s

The overthrow of Riza Shah put the country's international borders into question. In the north of Iran the occupation by the Soviet Union was accompanied by the pursuit of specific territorial objectives, which could be achieved only by the seizure of parts of north Iran.[7] After the end of hostilities Iran faced its first major challenge to its territorial integrity. In December 1946 an autonomous republic of Azerbaijan was declared in Tabriz under Ja'far Pishevari. The coup against the government in Tehran was underpinned by the presence of the armed forces of the USSR and was, it was feared in Tehran, to foreshadow the total loss of Azerbaijan to the USSR. Similar conclusions applied to the Kurdish People's Republic set up in Mahabad in west Iran in the same period. To many Western observers the establishment of the two autonomous republics was designed to move the Soviet frontier southwards in accordance with the objectives of the USSR as laid out in the Four Power Secret Pact of November 1940 between the USSR, Germany, Japan and Italy.[8]

The survival of Iran's 1941 frontier in the northwest was due to a combination of Iranian political adroitness and Western pressure on the USSR.[9] In January 1946 the government of the USSR refused to withdraw its armed forces from Iran, stating that its troops would remain in place until the originally agreed deadline of 2 March 1946. The Iranian government protested to the United Nations Security Council against Soviet prevarications. Help from that quarter was feeble and slow in forthcoming. It was left to the prime minister, Qavam Sultaneh, to fight the battle alone. He offered the USSR an oil agreement for the exploration in the five northern provinces – Asterabad, Azerbaijan, Gilan, Khorasan and Mazandaran – occupied in 1946 by Soviet troops, providing that their forces were withdrawn and subject to ratification of the oil concession by the *majlis* when it was reconvened. The matter was complemented by a British military landing near Basra and the start of a major tribal rebellion in the south of Iran supported by the British.[10]

In December 1946 the United States gave belated support to Qavam against the Soviet Union's attempt to rig the elections in Azerbaijan, which in effect ensured that Iranian government troops were enabled to enter Azerbaijan to supervise the elections for the *majlis* on 7 December. The, albeit late, Soviet withdrawal and the collapse of the Pishevari republic re-established Iranian sovereignty in the northwest and permitted a return to the pre-existing international boundaries in that region.

The revolution and the restatement of territorial integrity

It is important to note that none of the peripheral regions broke away from the Iranian state during the period of unrest in 1979–80 nor during the Iraqi invasions of 1980–1. This was in part a function of the internal cultural cohesion of the country and in part a result of prompt action by the central government to put down secessionist movements at their birth. At the same time, the development of Iran as a modern nation-state with a comparatively sophisticated economy in the period 1964–78 has brought about considerable rural–urban migration and trans-province movements to new work places. Together with a growth in national consciousness, these changes eroded traditional tribal and ethnic boundaries. For example, as many Azhari-origin people live outside northwest Iran as within it and the neat nature of the provinces as separate components of the state is increasingly misleading.

The only real danger for Iran from the remaining concentration of ethnic and linguistic minorities in its extreme borderlands is in Kurdistan, where an internationally sponsored Kurdish state would be very disruptive to the present balance where the majority Iranian Kurds see themselves ethnically as Kurds but also as citizens of Iran. At present, the Iranian, Turkish and Syrian governments recently and jointly have pledged themselves to maintain the territorial integrity of Iraq. The United States, France and the United Kingdom have also reassured the United Nations Security Council that Kurdistan will not be hived off as a separate state. The prospects for an autonomous Kurdish nation seem therefore to be very small on current evidence.[11]

Upheaval and recovery, 1979–88

The revolution of 1979 gave the opportunity for the ethnic groups to break away from the centre and to seek regional autonomy. In some regions there was unrest among the minorities during 1979 persisting throughout 1980. Marginal areas of the country were at times difficult of access by the government, which was unable to send its representatives, gather taxes or guarantee the security of the individual in parts of Azerbaijan, Kurdistan, Luristan, Fars, Khuzistan and the districts of the Persian Gulf. The most damaging insurrection occurred in Kurdistan, in so far as unrest was prolonged and widespread. The Kurdish rebellion persisted with isolated armed clashes between the Iranian security forces and Kurdish dissidents.

Some small-scale opposition, such as that by the Turkoman, was crushed early during 1979, though this was more a political movement of the left-wing *fedayin-e khalq* than an ethnic uprising. Arab separatist organizations in the oilfield province of Khuzistan were largely set up by and supported with arms supplies from Iraq. In Khuzistan, the linkage between the ethnic revolt and the problems of the oil industry was observed by one oil specialist: "the Arab population of Khuzistan . . . has been active in blowing up pipelines and in sabotage at refineries."[12] Under conditions of uncertainty in provincial areas, the British Foreign Office's off-the-record view was that "The question of territorial fission within Iran merits serious consideration".[13] Such judgements were not uncommon in the early 1980s in western Europe, Japan and North America and emphasize the insecurity, even as to the territorial unity of the country, during the period from February 1979 to September 1980.

The position after the revolution was, of course, exceptional and would not be expected to be repeated often. Under conditions of normality, Iran's border regions and ethnic minorities do not pose problems to internal security. Indeed, the revolutionary authorities were quick to suppress lawlessness in the border regions once the initial impact of the Iraqi invasions of Iranian soil had been turned. With exception of persistent though isolated unrest in Kurdistan, the country was returned to control by the central government in 1981.

Boundary affairs after 1988

The only shadow to arise in subsequent years was in late 1992 when proposals emanating from Baku for a united and independent Azerbaijan were published.[14] Claims for a united Azerbaijan raised memories in Tehran of the attempt in 1918 to establish an Azerbaijani National Council including within it Iranian Azerbaijan, which seemed at the time to be no more than a Turkish devised-means of separating it from Iran.[15] Official Iranian reactions in 1992 were also negative, as might have been expected. The notion of an integrated Azerbaijan was the first serious move from the areas of Transcaucasia and central Asia that suggested taking Iranian territories occupied by an ethnic or linguistic minority out of Iran. Throughout the early years of independence for the Transcaucasian and central Arabian republics no other cross-border territorial claims were made on Iran. But the prospect for other regional movements following the course taken by the Azerbaijan Republic gave an added dimension of insecurity to the northern border, quite at odds with the conventional wisdom of the day, which presupposed that Iran sought influence and territorial gain within the new republics at the expense of others.[16]

Iran as late as 1993 saw its new northern neighbours as Islamic co-religionists, as cultural allies and as trading partners. There was never any expression of territorial expansionism proclaimed by the Cabinet or the Ministry of Foreign Affairs, despite the occasional private speculation in the

Iranian academic community that Iran had historic claims to lands taken from it by imperial Russia in the 19th century. Iranian policies towards the central Asian and Caucasian republics were articulated through a series of cultural and commercial linkages, both bilateral and via the Economic Co-operation Organization (ECO)[17] or Caspian group.[18]

Iran's eastern borderlands gave rise to protracted negotiations between Iranian, Afghan and British interests during the 19th century.[19] In the recent period the only persistent problems in this area derived from the division of waters in the Sistan Basin, although maintaining the security of the Afghan frontier has been a constant difficulty in the face of smuggling and human migration, the latter at its peak during the Afghan–Soviet war in 1979–88.[20] It has been observed that boundary problems in Sistan arise generally in years of drought such as 1946 and 1971.[21] It should be added that years of heavy rainfall had the same effect through causing rivers on the line of the international boundary to change course, as for example in 1896 and the Iranian year 1902/3.[22] By 1992 the Iran/Afghan frontier was one of great activity as Iran sought the repatriation of some 2.7 million Afghan refugees.[23] Simultaneously the Iranian government also tried to end the smuggling of narcotics and other commodities into Iran and to reduce the permeability of the border region to Afghans seeking work in Iran.

Iran's western borders, inherited from the unsettled broad frontier zone of Persian–Ottoman imperial strife,[24] suffered varying fortunes in the modern period. The 1932 Agreement and the 1937 Convention, which fixed the alignment of the border between Iran and Turkey, caused continuing difficulties.[25] The years following the 1991 defeat of Iraq in Kuwait witnessed the Kurdish areas of Iraq falling under the protection of the United Nations and the emergence of a quasi-autonomous region governed by Kurdish people, signalled *inter alia* by the holding of elections in 1992.

The Iranian frontier with Turkey became subject to tensions in the modern period. The Iranian authorities were dismayed by infringements of Iranian territory by Turkish troops and aircraft in hot pursuit of Kurdish insurgents of the Kurdish Workers' Party (KKP). The Turkish government for its part appeared to believe that the KKP was using military bases in Iran as safe havens from which to launch guerrilla attacks on Turkish villages and border posts.[26] The matter was temporarily resolved in November 1992 at a trilateral meeting in Ankara where Iranian, Turkish and Syrian foreign ministers agreed that the territorial integrity of Iraq would not be undermined by any of the three neighbours. Separate bilateral arrangements were also made for improved security and a cessation of Kurdish border crossings between Iran, Turkey and northern Iraq.

Iran's border with Iraq remained profoundly unstable in the modern period.[27] Three great areas of dispute have been at the heart of the problem: first, the Shatt al-Arab boundary; secondly, the land frontier around Penjwin and border post 101; and, thirdly, the offshore zone at the head of the Persian Gulf. Naturally, the Shatt al-Arab international boundary dispute attracted most attention[28] since it has been both a *casus belli* and a battlefront within recent years.[29] The apparent renunciation of the 1975 Accord on the Shatt al-Arab by Iran in June 1979 and Iraq in October 1979 indicated the fragility of the frontier zone. Grounds for continuing tensions in this area can be discerned in the failure of mediators of the United Nations Organization to get Iraq to ratify the provisions of UN Resolution 598, on which the Iran–Iraq ceasefire of 1988 was agreed. In the immediate aftermath of the war it appeared that Iraq would use its strong bargaining position vis-à-vis a militarily and economically weakened Iran to press for the international boundary along the Shatt al-Arab to revert to that provided for under the 1937 Agreement, fixing the line on the low- water mark on the Iranian side of the river.[30] Iran naturally resisted Iraqi overtures to this end and demanded that the frontier return to the *status quo ante* September 1980, which was the Iranian interpretation of the wording of UN Resolution 598.

Events took a further radical turn in 1990 following the invasion of Kuwait by Iraqi forces. Iraqi representatives offered Iran a full and absolute reversion of the border along the Shatt al-Arab to the position accepted under the 1975 Accord. Other components of the Iraqi offer to Iran were ratification of a peace agreement under the terms of Resolution 598, the return of all prisoners of war, normalization of economic and diplomatic relations and complete withdrawal of Iraqi troops behind the 1980 frontiers. In return, Iran was presumably to accept the *de facto* integration of Kuwait into Iraq. The Iranian authorities did not accede to the Iraqi proposals and continued to demand that Iraq withdraw from Kuwaiti territory as a prelude to a negotiated settlement of the issue. Iranian attempts to mediate an Iraqi withdrawal from Kuwait were rebuffed by Saddam Hussain, despite the clear desire in Tehran for a peaceful settlement, which would obviate the need for a military solution by the UN coalition led by the United States. The 1988 arrangements for a settlement of the Shatt al-Arab dispute thus came to nothing during 1990–1. In 1992 the USA and its coalition partners set up a "no-flying" zone in the south of Iraq to protect the Shi'ite community from air attack by the central government, thereby forestalling any Irano–Iraqi agreement that might have been reached. Meanwhile, Khorramshahr port was opened to river traffic in December 1992, with Iran utilizing full rights to navigation on the Shatt al-Arab in the absence of an agreement with Iraq.[31]

Elsewhere on the Iran/Iraq borderlands, tensions were exacerbated by the inability of the Iraqi central government to enforce security. Kurdish groups were active throughout the border area and the Iranian authorities continued to support Iraqi opposition groups in SAIRI (Supreme Assembly of the Islamic Revolution of Iraq), in effect making the Iran/Iraq frontier very permeable. Iranian aircraft attacked Iraqi territory in April 1992 in an attempt to bomb the headquarters of the mujahidin-i khalq organization (MKO). Both countries made recurrent protests to the UN on the matter of border violations throughout the early 1990s.

It is apparent that the Iran/Iraq border remains prone to deep problems. In part these frictions along the international frontier reflect underlying political problems between the rather different regimes in Tehran and Baghdad.[32] It might be observed with justification that some of the problems affecting the frontier areas also derive from rather deeper-seated difficulties arising from specifically geographical phenomena. There are, for example, the fraught questions of family, tribal and religious groups that are divided by the international border,[33] together with the long-term involvement of these same peoples in smuggling, armed raiding and drug trafficking. At the same time, the specific issues of control of navigation and sovereignty on the Shatt al-Arab remain to bedevil relations, however good general diplomatic links might or might not be.[34] The geography of southern Iraq where it abuts onto the Persian Gulf in a restricted shoreline of a few tens of kilometres is out of proportion to so large and rich a hinterland. Even the most unsympathetic observer of Iraq was moved to the conclusion on Iraq's limited access to the waters of the Persian Gulf that "Iraq has never come to accept the harsh reality of its geographic predicament in relation to the Gulf."[35] Ancel's postulate that "There are no problems of boundaries. There are only problems of nations,"[36] seems in these circumstances to be largely inapplicable, therefore, to the question of the conflict over the Shatt al-Arab boundary and even to confrontations over considerable lengths of the Iran/Iraq land frontier.

The Iranian frontage to the Persian Gulf, like that on the Shatt al-Arab, has remained in a state of partial flux. The majority of agreements concerning division of the continental shelf have proved to be viable – notably those with Saudi Arabia, Oman, Qatar and Bahrain. Other areas of the continental shelf have either not been subject to existing treaties or are affected by disputes over earlier agreements. An example of the former situation can be seen at the head of the Persian Gulf, where, as noted earlier, Iran, Iraq and Kuwait have failed to finalize division of the so-called "golden triangle". Acrimonious and capricious argument has characterized a number of offshore settlements, none more so than those between Iran and Sharjah and between Iran and Ras al-Khaimah. Here two powerful undercurrents are discernible, one deriving from generic insecurity and suspicion between the respective governments working within the concept laid down by Ancel and another arising from specific local matters of sovereignty and strategic control.

The contemporary history of Abu Musa illustrates the volatility surrounding frontiers where there is chronic and latent dissatisfaction on both sides concerning the "fairness" and "legitimacy" of an existing boundary settlement. The Abu Musa issue is dealt with by Pirouz Mojtahed-Zadeh in Chapter 9. It must be emphasized, however, that there has been an episodic recurrence of difficulties that augurs badly for future stability. The nub of the local problem is one of sovereignty and the rival Iranian and Sharjawi claims to the island. The *de facto* shared control since 1971 has tended to confirm the Iranian belief that it has sovereignty on an equal and shared footing with Sharjah, while the authorities in Sharjah appear to view the 1971 settlement as allocating sovereignty to Sharjah but rights of military usufruct to Iran. The legal basis for the claims of the two sides in the dispute will eventually have to be examined by an impartial arbitrator or a separate political agreement reached. In the interim, Abu Musa has become a *cause célèbre* at the Middle Eastern regional level as a symbol of Arab national resistance to the spread of Iranian influence in the Persian Gulf. This status, which will also be found to apply to the islands of Greater Tunb and Lesser Tunb, has been a continuing theme since 1971, sparking Arab consciousness of wrong done to the greater Arab nation (Qoum al-Arabiyah) as far away as Libya, where British Petroleum's assets in Concession 65 were nationalized in 1971 in protest at alleged British government complicity in the Iranian seizure of the islands.

Iraq adopted the issue of the Iranian military occupation of the Gulf islands in setting out its case for attacking Iran in September 1980. In 1992 the same theme was raised again by the United Arab Emirates in response to the unfortunate incidents on Abu Musa, which included the expulsion of workers from Sharjah and returning school teachers in September 1992. By the end of 1992 the Abu Musa dispute had taken on a regional if not international rôle in which the Iranian tenancy of the Persian Gulf islands was being put into question. More threatening for Iran, the dispute over Abu Musa became inextricably linked with that of sovereignty of the Tunb islands and Iran's entire strategy towards the Persian Gulf was put into question.[37]

Notes

1. K. S. McLachlan, "Borders in the Ottoman Empire", in *Encyclopaedia Iranica*, E. Yarshater (ed.), 401 (London: Routledge, 1989).
2. H. Arfa, *Under five shahs*, 111–85 (London: John Murray, 1964).
3. D. N. Wilber, *Iran*, 126 (Princeton: Princeton University Press, 1976).
4. R. Ferrier, *The history of the British Petroleum company*, vol. 1, 632–5 (Cambridge: Cambridge University Press, 1982); J. Marlowe, *Iran: a short political guide*, 55–7 (London: Pall Mall, 1963).
5. W. E. Griffith, "Iran's foreign policy", in *Iran under the Pahlavis*, G. Lenczowski (ed.), 370–1 (Stanford: Hoover Institute, 1978).
6. Wilber, op. cit., 132.
7. Marlowe, op. cit., 71.
8. M. Sicker, *The bear and the lion*, 55 (New York: Praeger, 1988).

9. R. W. Cottam, *Nationalism in Iran*, 198 (Pittsburgh: University of Pittsburgh Press, 1964).
10. R. N. Fry, *Iran*, 87 (London: Allen & Unwin, 1954).
11. cf. M. T. O'Shea, Chapter 5.
12. F. Fesharaki, *Revolution and energy policy in Iran*, 25 (London: Economist Intelligence Unit, 1980).
13. Unpublished paper of the Tripartite seminar (1981), School of Oriental and African Studies, University of London, cf. paper of 14 October 1981.
14. *Tehran Times*, 27 December 1992.
15. T. Swietochowski, *Russian Azerbaijan 1905-20: the shaping of national identity in a Muslim community*, 129-30 (Cambridge: Cambridge University Press, 1985).
16. "Iran seeks silken ties with central Asian neighbours", *Financial Times*, 22 June 1992.
17. "Iran's relations with the southern members of the CIS", *Background brief*, 2-3 (London: Foreign and Commonwealth Office, 1992).
18. cf. Abbas Maleki, Chapter 2.
19. P. Mojtahed-Zadeh, "The evolution of the eastern Iranian boundaries: the rôle of the Khozeimeh amirdom". PhD thesis (Department of Geography, School of Oriental and African Studies, 1993).
20. D. Balland, "The borders of Afghanistan", in Yarshater, op. cit., 413-14.
21. Ibid.
22. Ibid., 413; Mojtahed-Zadeh, op. cit.
23. *Iran Focus* 6 (1993), 5-6.
24. McLachlan, op. cit., 401-3.
25. R. N. Schofield, "Iran's borders with Turkey", in Yarshater, op. cit., 418.
26. *Iran Monitor* 8 (1992), 4-5.
27. S. Chubin & C. Tripp, *Iran and Iraq at war* (London: I. B. Tauris, 1988).
28. R. N. Schofield, *The evolution of the Shatt al-Arab boundary dispute* (London: Menas Press, 1986).
29. K. S. McLachlan & E. G. H. Joffé, *The Gulf war: a survey of political issues and economic consequences* (London: Economic Intelligence Unit, 1984).
30. E. G. H. Joffé & K. S. McLachlan, *Iran and Iraq: building on the stalemate*, 3-4 (London: Economist Intelligence Unit, 1988).
31. *Iran Monitor* 1 (1993), 24.
32. G. Balfour-Paul, "The prospects for peace", in *The Iran-Iraq war*, M. S. Azhary (ed.), 126-7 (London: Croom Helm, 1984).
33. Lord Kendal, "The Kurds under the Ottoman Empire", in *People without a country: the Kurds and Kurdistan*, G. Chaliand (ed.), 43 (London: Zed Books, 1978).
34. A. Cordesman, "The regional balance", in *The Gulf war*, H. Maul & O. Pick (eds), 85 (London: Pinter, 1989).
35. D. Finnie, *Shifting lines in the sand: Kuwait's elusive frontier with Iraq*, 175 (London: I. B. Tauris, 1992).
36. J. Ancel, *Les frontières*, 196 (Paris: Galliard, 1936).
37. cf. K. S. McLachlan, Chapter 6.

CHAPTER TWO

Iran's northeastern borders
From Sarakhs to Khazar (the Caspian Sea)

ABBAS MALEKI

Introduction

In the pre-Islamic and post-Arab invasion periods, the Iranian frontiers were further to the northeast than at present, comprising the Oxus (Amu-Darya) and Iaxartes (Syr-Darya) rivers, and the Transoxiana (Mavara-ol-Nahr) region. Later, during the Qajar period, Iran's land area shrank considerably, and, based on the 1921 treaty, the present Sarakhs/Khazar border was eventually established (Fig. 2.1).

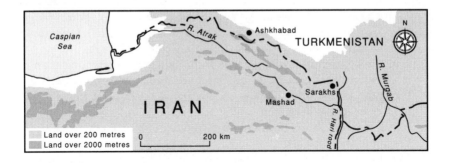

Figure 2.1 Iran's northeastern borders from the Sarakhs to the Caspian, 1993.

Throughout the era of communist control in the former Soviet Union, this border functioned as an "iron wall". It could be crossed only in exceptional cases. With the advent of *perestroika* and *glasnost*, and the recent developments under Gorbachev's leadership, communism has collapsed. In the context of its good relations with neighbouring states, *inter alia* the former Soviet Union, the Islamic Republic of Iran attempted to expand Irano–Soviet politico–diplomatic ties in a bid to enhance the cultural and economic dimensions of these relations. This step has been greatly encouraged by the people of the central Asian republics. Hence, owing to the willingness and goodwill of both nations, a Memorandum of Understanding was signed in 1990 on the area of permitted access for persons crossing the frontier (45 km deep on each side). Subsequent to this landmark event, and given the earnest desire of the people of the central Asian republics, bilateral relations along this border have expanded. Obviously, given the unfolding developments, the future of this border will be tremendously different. It will be transformed to a border of understanding, communication and, ultimately, co-operation. It is within this framework that the situation of and the economic life in border cities will start to assume importance. In order to amplify this situation a brief review will be provided later on key towns and cities situated on the Iranian side of the Khazar/Sarakhs border, together with an analysis of the current situation in the republic of Turkmenistan.

Historical overview of the northeastern border region

"Border" is a political term that designates the territorial limit of a state. And, whenever this term is applied to Iran in an evolutionary sense, the "plateau" of Iran is the first thing that comes to mind.

The Iranian plateau covers an area of $2,600,000 km^2$ and lies between the Caspian Sea – Kharazm plain and the Persian Gulf – Oman Sea. It embodies the Zagros ranges to the west, Arvand (Shatt al-Arab) river, Pamir ranges and the Oxus to the northeast. In the vortex of history, Iran's topography has shaped this country's characteristics in a number of ways:

(a) Iran's geographical position made it the bridge for communication by land between far eastern Asia, China and India, and the African and European lands. This claim is substantiated by the fact that the Silk road crossed northern Iran.

(b) Iran is situated in the northern hemisphere, with an equal reach to the West and the Far East.

(c) This plateau enjoys perennial streams and rivers: Oxus and Iaxartes to the northeast, Punjab and Sind to the east and southeast, Euphrates and Tigris to the west. Flowing in the four corners of the Iranian plateau, these rivers have historically encouraged the burgeoning of civilizations along their banks.

However, these same characteristics have also carried misfortune for the Iranian plateau, for they transformed it into a major bone of contention for warriors and aggressors who, regardless of their origins, incessantly aspired to control Iranian territory. An overview of the history of the borders, especially the northeastern borders, would attest to this fact.[1]

The first Aryan entry into Iran occurred about half way through the second millennium BC. The first Iranian state was founded by one of the Aryan tribes; the bounds of this state extended northeastward near the

Oxus river. It was during the Achaemenid (Hakhamanashian) dynasty that the empire further expanded, encompassing in the northeast Ghorasmia, Sughd, Scythian territories and Bactria, which included Merv.

Under the Arsacids and the Sassanians Iran's boundaries were further stabilized and the northeastern borders retreated inward towards the Oxus, but the cultural borders still extended to Iaxartes.

With the advent of Islam and the defeat of the Sassanians (AD 637), Iran was ruled for two centuries by the Umaiyad and the Abbasid caliphates. During this era, Transoxiana was situated immediately beyond the northeastern border. Subsequent to the Arab invasion, local dynasties emerged one after the other: the Tahirids (821), the Saffarids (867), the Samanids (874), the Ziyarids (920s), and the Buyids (932).

Two kinds of political borders started to emerge, one separating the local dynasties, and the other separating the Arabs from the Iranians. As to the northeastern borders in this period, one has to note that Transoxiana was ruled by the Samanids and the Ashro–Sand region by the Tahirids. During the Saffarid reign, the Oxus and Iaxartes emerged as the northeastern and eastern borders of Iran respectively.

With Ghengis (1160) and Hulegu (1245) leading the Mongol hordes across the breadth of Iran, the five-century old caliphate was terminated. The rule of Khwarazmshahs came to its end and the Il-Khanids came to the throne. In this period, the heirs of Ghengis continued their conquests and Iran's northeastern limits were further extended to include Transoxiana and east and west Turkmenistan. On the other side, the Oxus still delimited the territories of these two families.

It was during the Timurid dynasty and Shah Abbas's reign that a large portion of Iran was governed by a central government, and regions such as Balkh, Merv, Herat and Qandahar together formed Iran's northeastern frontier. The Oxus separated Iran and the Ozbeg kingdom in Central Asia.

After assuming power, and being a military genius, Nadir Shah marched into the heart of India and reconquered Qandahar, which was lost at the end of the Safavid dynasty.

Hence, it can be noted that during Nadir's reign the northeastern and eastern limits of Iran extended considerably. Nadir thoroughly understood the significance of an effective naval power and founded a number of maritime bases on the Caspian Sea and the Persian Gulf.

Nadir's death was once again followed by a scramble for the throne and a period of political rivalries among local dynasties. Karim Khan Zand attempted to stabilize the borders, but his heirs engaged in heavy internal feuds. With the Zands weakened, Agha Muhammad Khan Qajar founded the Qajar dynasty. During the Qajar reign the country plunged into the abyss of foreign intervention, culminating in Iran's territorial dismemberment.

In retrospect, throughout Iran's ancient history and even after the Arab invasion, with the exception of a number of brief periods, Iran's northeastern borders extended to the Oxus, the Iaxartes and the central Asian region.

During the Qajar period, the first treaty signed between Iran and Tsarist Russia was the 1813 Treaty of Gulistan. The treaty was signed after nine consecutive years of Irano–Russian war, which aimed at bringing northern Iran, specifically Georgia, under Russian control. In the village of Gulistan, near Qarabagh, representatives from each of the two countries signed the treaty on 12 October 1813.[2]

Fifteen years later, after 18 months of Irano–Russian war, which resulted in the military defeat of Iran, the Treaty of Turkmanchai was signed in the village of Turkmanchai in the vicinity of Tabriz on 22 February 1828.[3] The Treaty of Turkmanchai replaced the Treaty of Gulistan. Under this instrument Russia acquired the northern Iranian provinces of Erivan and Nakhchivan beyond the Araxes. Iran was also compelled to pay an indemnity of 20 million roubles. The treaty granted rights of passage to Iranian and Russian commercial ships on the Caspian and Russian exclusivity to maintain a navy on those waters.

During this period, a system of extraterritorial legal rights and privileges was accorded without reservation to the Tsarist government. The Russian presence along the Caspian Sea and the occupation of a number of islands incited dissent among Turkmens, e.g. the Iranian Turkmens who resided in Iran and/or the Russian Turkmens. The Russians also manipulated the Iranian Yamut Turkmens to rise against the Iranian government, an act greatly deplored by the latter.[4]

Finally, to prevent Turkmen invasions and border disturbances, in 1900, a joint Irano–Russian commission was founded in Gonbad Qabus. The Turkmens lived along the Gorgan/Sarakhs border, an area adjacent to northern Khorasan. Historically, the Turkmens had been particularly prone to raid Iran. At times even the Turkmen border-settlers at Merv incited disturbances and skirmishes.

Fifty years after the signing of the Turkmanchai treaty, Russia extended its borders and acquired Tashkent, Bokhara, Samarqand and Turkmenistan. In 1902, Russian military forces occupied Sarakhs, which was annexed to Asterabad, thereafter renamed as the "Old Sarakhs" and the "Russian Sarakhs".

In 1904, Nasser-al Din Shah ordered that the "New Sarakhs" or the "Nasserite Sarakhs" be founded. More than 300 families settled in the vicinity of the New Sarakhs, which were situated to the west of the Tajan river. Hotels and military bases were also established. To the east of the Tajan more than 2,300 Turkmen families and tribes were settled. The majority were Russian nationals, engaged in notable feuds with the Iranians over the use of the river, hence restricting the latter's access to water. In the aftermath of these disturbances, transit and postal facilities were transferred from Sarakhs to Bajgiran.[5]

In 1907, the Anglo–Russian Convention was signed. This instrument provided for the partition of Iran into spheres of influence, with Russia in the north (including the Khazar/Sarakhs border region), Britain in the south and west, and a neutral buffer zone between the two powers. From this period onwards, Russia's high-handed policy in its sphere of influence and the Khazar/Sarakhs border region became conspicuous.

Russian attitudes and policies remained unaltered until the 1917 October revolution. Finally, on 26 February 1921, the Soviet–Iranian Treaty of Friendship was signed in Moscow by the Soviet foreign minister, Chicherin, his deputy, Karkhan, and the Iranian ambassador to Moscow, Dr Ansari. The instrument was ratified in August 1921 by the USSR's Central Committee and subsequently by the Iranian *majlis*. The Turkmanchai treaty was duly abrogated.[6] The 1921 Treaty of Friendship provided both parties equal rights to navigation on the Caspian Sea. Nonetheless, the Old Sarakhs remained under Russian control. To settle the question of the use of frontier waters, representatives from Iran, Turkmenistan and the Soviet Union worked out additional agreements in 1922 and 1926 on the basis of the 1921 treaty, which governs border relations between the two countries to this day.

Hence, during the Qajar period, Iran's area shrank to its minimum, and the northeastern border (Khazar/Sarakhs) was established on the basis of the 1921 treaty and the ensuing agreements. The 1921 treaty provided for the settlement of all border disputes between Iran and the Soviet Union. Under its terms, Ashuradeh island and the rural village of Firouzeh were to be transferred to Iran. However, Firouzeh still remains under the control of the Turkmen government.

Recent developments on the northeastern border: the Iranian borderlands and the republic of Turkmenistan[7]

The main cities situated along the Khazar/Sarakhs border are: Bandar Turkmen, Gorgan (Asterabad), Gonbad, Bojnurd, Shirvan, Quchan, Mashad, and the border villages of Agh-Ghala, Gomeishan, Doshli Borun, Chat, Maraveh Tappeh, Raz, Bajgiran (now Khandan), Lotf Abad, Kabud Gonbad, and Sarakhs. The main link towns through which intercommunication occurs between Iran and the former Soviet Union are (from west to east): the Pol border station in Doshli Borun district, Bajgiran, Lotf Abad and Sarakhs.

Bandar Turkmen, Doshli Borun and the Pol border station
In ancient times this region was named Hirekani or Asterabad. It is situated to the southeast of the Caspian Sea between the Atrek and Qarasu rivers. The region's altitude is relatively low, while small hills such as Tappeh Kolah and Takhmagh, together with shifting river beds, alter the region's geographical configuration.

The majority of the permanent settlers in this area (who used to be trans-humant tribes) are of Turkmen descent and have preserved their traditional lifestyle. They engage in cattle-raising, agriculture and fishery. Carpet-weaving and horse-breeding are amongst their traditional chores.

Bandar Turkmenis enjoy the necessary public services, e.g. liquid gas dis-tribution, clean water, electricity, health and cultural centres. The port's population has reached 110,000, comprising such tribes as Yomut, Gukalan and Takeh. Bandar Turkmen's agricultural products comprise cereals, cotton and dairy products, and along the Caspian coast fishing is the primary source of income. The commercial and industrial institutions of this port in-clude a fishing installation on Ashuradeh island and a train wagon repair factory in Bandar Turkmen.

The main transit points in this area are (from west to east): Makhdum Gholi, western Sangar Tappeh, Sufi-Kom, the Pol station and Chat. These areas are linked by railways and roads. The majority of the inhabitants are Hanafi Muslims. Given recent developments in Irano–Soviet relations, the settlers in the areas adjacent to the border have expressed inclinations to cross the border. This factor has been enhanced further by tribal, religious, cultural and historical factors. Recent visitors to Turkmenistan have revealed that the settlers of that region are even more eager to cross the border into Iran. Their desire has been intensified by the long period of subjugation and the recent collapse of the communist dictatorship. The people are attracted by a host of historical, tribal, economic and social factors in Iran and await the opening of the border in order positively to draw upon the wealth of Iranian culture. As regards the Turkmen cultural heritage in Iran, the tomb of Makhdum Gholi, the Turkmen poet who lived in this area 200 years ago, is worthy of mention. On the other hand, President Nyazev's successful official visit to Iran in October 1991 was another parameter contributing to Turkmens' eagerness to cross the border into Iran.

The Pol border station, now on the verge of opening, is situated in Doshli Borun district, which is a semi-desert area with Injeh Borun as its main centre. Doshli Borun and its 33 surrounding villages together have a popula-tion of 33,000. The inhabitants enjoy public services – electricity, water, li-quid gas distribution, schools and health centres. Roads link this area to other regions. Lakes cover a portion of this border region, some of which have been included in an environmental protection plan: Alagol pond, Ton-goli and Hajigol. Gudry station is situated across from Pol station and the border posts have facilitated the crossing of the frontier by settlers since 15 February 1990.

The locational advantage of Pol and Doshli Borun could turn this zone into an active transit point, hence playing a constructive rôle in the two countries' cultural, economic and social exchanges.

The town of Quchan and the Bajgiran frontier

Quchan is situated to the northwest of Mashad at an altitude of 1217 m and comprises an area of 6900 km². The abundance of rivers and valleys increases the significance of this region in such realms as agriculture and cattle-raising. Given its links with Mashad, the Soviet border and Iran's northern highways, Quchan's economy and commerce have flourished. Its revenue is mainly derived from the production of cereals, fruits, raisins, dairy products and handicrafts (e.g. carpets and furs). This town, surrounded by 15 counties and 625 villages, has a population of 100,000–250,000 when the population of districts is factored in.[8]

Bajgiran is one of this area's districts. The nearest border station is 600 km away from Quchan. The region is 100 per cent mountainous with cold winters and pleasant summers; temperature ranges from −10°C to 25°C, with an average precipitation of 120 mm.

Bajgiran has two districts and 180 surrounding villages, the most important of which are Shamkhal, Bardar and Qarajiqeh. This zone has been historically important as far as Irano–Russian communications were concerned, hence its elaborate border and transit installations. The indigenous population consists mainly of Kurds and Shi'ites. When the borders were closed, the population of this zone plunged from 3500 to 1000 families. Nonetheless, after the recent revitalization of border areas and settler crossings, Bajgiran is witnessing a new period of renaissance. The border station is currently being developed and expanded to meet the commercial and import/export needs of both sides.[9]

Lotf Abad

Lotf Abad is another transit point situated to the west of Sarakhs in the Dargaz province. This province is to the north of the Hizar Panjeh ranges. The railway crossing at Lotf Abad has tremendously increased the significance of this transit point.

Sarakhs

Sarakhs is situated 180 km to the east of Mashad, exactly on the Irano/Turkmen border. Its altitude ranges between 250 m and 1950 m, its temperature between −20° and 40°C, and it has an average precipitation of 200 mm. The area is irrigated by such rivers as Tajan (Harirud) and underground waters. It is a prominent region in terms of agriculture and cattle-raising, with its agricultural products comprising cereals, fruits, summer crops and pistachios.[10]

The abundance of natural gas in the Sarakhs region and the Khangiran gas refinery 22 km to the west have brought about considerable change in the civil and industrial fabric of this thriving region. The gas reserves in Sarakhs are estimated at 21.5 trillion m³. Thus far only eight wells have been explored with a capacity of 60 million m³ per day.

The Sarakhs region embodies six villages, 76 rural districts and a population of 58,000 – mostly Sistanis, Baluchis, Zabolis, Turkmens and Arabs (60 per cent of whom are Shi'ite and 40 per cent Sunni).[11] A few kilometres away from the Iranian Sarakhs lies the Soviet Sarakhs on the eastern bank of the Tajan river. Meanwhile, the historical sites of Merv and Bokhara are the nearest cities to Sarakhs.

The republic of Turkmenistan

The republic of Turkmenistan covers an area of 488,100 km^2 and has a population of 3.7 million. The population configuration of this region is 72 per cent Turkmen, 10 per cent Russian, 9 per cent Uzbek and 33 per cent Kazakh. The majority of Turkmens are Hanafi Muslims. Ashkhabad is the capital, with a population of 400,000. It is situated to the north of the Kopeh Dagh ranges, 45 km from Bajgiran.

Crosnovdosk is the most important sea port in Turkmenistan. Other important cities and/or towns include: Chardash, with a population of 146,000, and Neibat-Dagh, Beirum-Ali, Chalkan, Binkan, Merv, Qazal-Arvat and Tajan, each with populations below 100,000.

The republic is endowed with a wealth of natural resources and exports 80 billion m^3 of natural gas per year.

During recent developments in the former Soviet Union, Turkmenistan underwent a relatively peaceful transition, largely due to its current president, Morad Nyazev, who seems to have a good command of the republic's internal situation.

The Qara Qum (Black Sand) plain covers an area of 375,000 km^2 in this republic and includes such regions as Geli Murdeh. Irrigation canals (1000 km) supply water to 850,000 hectares of land, while 95,000 peasants are involved in the agricultural sector. In 1992, 1.3 million tons of cotton were produced. Precipitation averages 80 mm per year and, in higher altitude regions, it can reach 300 mm per year.

Recently, Turkmen officials have revised the republic's agricultural policies. They plan to produce other needed products internally and to become self-sufficient in wheat production.

Concluding remarks

Iran's northeastern border from the Caspian to the Sarakhs has always been the cradle of Islamic and Iranian civilizations and sciences. The emergence of literary and scientific elites attests to this fact – including figures such as Ferdowsi, Khayyam Neishaburi, Anwari, Ghazali, Khajeh Nassir-al-Din Tusi, Abdollah Jeyhani, Abolfazl Bal'ami, Avecenna, Rudaki, Abu Reyhan Biruni, Khwarazmi, Sarakhsi and Sanaei Ghaznavi.

In addition to its rich cultural heritage, this region has been a main cata-lyst for national, historical and cultural links among Turkmen and/or Kurd-ish settlers and tribes. Throughout the years, these tribes were instrumental in preserving the territorial integrity of Iran.

In more recent times the Irano–Turkmen ties have improved and bilateral relations are bringing the two countries closer. With the conclusion of the 15 February 1990, 7 August 1990 and 22 September 1991 Memoranda of Understanding between the Islamic Republic of Iran and the Soviet Union, settlers can cross the borders 45 km deep on each side and engage in com-mercial activities in such areas as Bajgiran.

According to the 15 February 1990 Memorandum of Understanding, set-tlers of the border regions can either walk or drive across the frontier four times per year. To facilitate their passage, 11 transit points were selected, four of which are in the northeastern border area. The memorandum is valid for a period of three years and, should none of the parties require its abrogation, it will be extended automatically every three years. The two sig-natories to the memorandum agreed that the Bajgiran/Gavdan border be opened on 22 September 1991. Facilities for the opening of other transit points were also provided for in this instrument.

In December 1991 the Iranian foreign minister, Ali Akbar Velayati, led a high-ranking delegation to visit the central Asian republics during which he signed a Memorandum of Understanding on greater Irano–Turkmen scientif-ic, cultural, economic and political co-operation in Ashkhabad. The symbol of Irano–Turkmen co-operation was crystallized in the Tajan–Mashad rail-way, the Tajan–Sarakhs portion of which is currently under construction in the republic of Turkmenistan. On the Iranian side, preliminary studies are under way for the construction of the Sarakhs–Mashad line. Once the Turk-men and Iranian railways are linked, the line will start from the port of Shanghai in the Pacific, and pass through northern China, Kazakhstan, Kirghizia, Tajikistan, Uzbekistan and Turkmenistan. The line will join the Iranian rail network through to Turkey and Europe.[12]

It is hoped that in the near future the ground for greater multilateral ex-change will be paved. Relations between Iran and the central Asian repub-lics are on the verge of a new era of transparency of frontiers and expansion of communication, which should foster greater understanding and cultural exchange. As such, human civilization can constructively evolve so as to solidify the foundations of regional peace and friendship. Fortunately, since time immemorial, Iran has played a constructive cultural rôle that has trans-cended international frontiers in central Asia and that should provide a strong basis for an expansion in Iranian links with to that area.

Notes

1. Information on the history of Iranian boundaries was extracted from the following sources: Ahmad Behmanish, Mohammad-Ibrahim Bastani & Issa Behnam (eds), *The historical atlas of Iran* (Tehran: Tehran University, 1971); Mohammad-Ali Mukhbir, *The Iranian borders*,1-4, 8-22 (Tehran: Keyhan, 1945); Hassan Pirnia, *The ancient history of Iran*, 545 (Tehran: Donyayae Kitab, 1983).

2. Lisan-ol-Molk Sepehr, *Nassikh-ol-Tavarikh*, vol. 1, 4470 (Tehran: Islamieh, 1978).

3. Ibrahim Safaiee, *One hundred historical documents*, 65 (Tehran: History Association of Iran, 1977).

4. Sepehr, op. cit., vol. 2, 6.

5. Ibrahim Safaiee, *Qajar political documents*, 166-77 (Tehran: Sharq Publications, 1967).

6. File no. 64, Chapter 30, Documents from the Iranian Ministry of Foreign Affairs (1921).

7. Information on the cities along the Khazar/Sarakhs border was gathered by researchers from the Institute for Political and International Studies, who visited the area in October 1991.

8. Ramazan-Ali Shakeri, *A comprehensive history of Quchan*, 19-39 (Tehran: Amir Kabir, 1985).

9. Ibid.

10. Ahmad Ranjbar, *The great Khorassan*, 149-55 (Tehran: Amir Kabir, 1983).

11. Ibid., 155-9.

12. *Etela'at*, 14 December 1991, 3.

CHAPTER THREE

Nomads and commissars on the frontiers of eastern Azerbaijan

RICHARD TAPPER

Preamble

Until modern times, frontiers were not about territory and lines and colours on maps. In Iran, as in other pre-modern states, territory of itself was of little interest to rulers at any level – they were more concerned with controlling populations who could exploit the territory and provide a source of revenue and military manpower.

The preferred method of doing this was to settle people of trusted loyalty on the frontiers. Alternatively, a strong ruler would make sure to tour the frontier marches that he claimed, personally, or vicariously by means of trusted agents, in order to beat the bounds, to impress the inhabitants, to collect revenues, by force if necessary, to reward loyalty and to punish disloyalty.[1] In extreme cases, strong rulers like Abbas I Safavi or Nadir Afshar would resort to policies such as the forced migration of whole populations or creating a "scorched-earth" frontier zone.

Cheaper, but less effective and less productive, was to recognize local leaders, by appointing them as local governors or chiefs, ensuring their loyalty by keeping members of their family at court as hostages. This was common policy in the 18th century and much of the 19th century. The Qajars additionally appointed relatives as local governors in the not always justified belief that this was a guarantee of both loyalty and revenue.

The southeastern Caucasus and the Azerbaijan frontier

The southeastern Caucasus has always offered a highly favourable environment for both pastoral and agricultural activities. High mountains, with abundant summer pasturages, command the vast and fertile Shirvan, Qarabagh (Mil) and Moghan plains of the lower Aras and Kor rivers, which provide correspondingly extensive winter grazing. The plains also invite the

21

construction of large-scale irrigation works, such as those completed by Tamerlane in Moghan, which seem to have continued in operation throughout Safavid times.

The plains were a favourite wintering place of conquerors, while not surprisingly the whole area was long the object of intense struggle between powerful states. The Safavids gained control at the beginning of the 16th century, but had difficulty keeping it from the Ottomans, the Russians and various Caucasian powers, and when the dynasty crumbled in the early 18th century the area was divided briefly between the Ottomans and the Russians. After a further 80 years of Iranian hegemony, it was the Russians who annexed most of the area for good.

The area is also a natural crossroads, and trade and travel between Russia and Iran and between Anatolia and central Asia passed through or close by. From Safavid times, travellers and merchants from Europe commonly journeyed overland through Russia and took ship on the Caspian, to land at Shirvan and halt awhile at the growing trading centre of Shamakhi, before crossing the Kor at the Javat bridge[2] and passing via Moghan and Ardabil into central Iran, and beyond to India.

Of the several excellent pastoral nomad habitats that centre on this area, the only one still left in Iranian territory is the part of Azerbaijan that stretches from the Savalan, Bzkush and Baghrou mountains around Ardabil northwards to the plains of Moghan. This is of course the habitat now associated with the Shahsevan, one of the major Iranian tribal confederations of recent times. While the other plains fell within the provinces of Qarabagh and Shirvan, the Moghan steppe south of the Aras and Kor seems at times to have been included in the Azerbaijan province.

East Azerbaijan under the Safavids

The present frontier region in eastern Azerbaijan was central to the emergence of the Safavid dynasty in the 15th and early 16th centuries, as has been many times recounted; particularly in the events of Shah Ismail I's early life. Ardabil was the shrine of the founder of the Safavid order, Shaikh Safi, and remained holy to the Safavids though they located their capital not there but in Tabriz and then Isfahan.

Before Safavid times, the population of eastern Azerbaijan was probably a mixture, or an alternation, of Kurdish, Turkic, Mongol and other elements. The Kurdish groups, and others speaking Iranian languages, were autochthonous, while the Turks and Mongols were comparative newcomers.

Shirvan and Ardabil were governed for the early Safavids by Qizilbash chiefs from a variety of tribal groups, who presumably had large numbers of their followers living a pastoral life in the vicinity. There were apparently extensive irrigated farmlands on the lower reaches of the Kor around Salyan.

The Ottomans occupied Shirvan from 1579 to 1607, and much of Azerbaijan from 1585 to 1603. By the treaty of 1591–2, Shah Abbas held them to the west of Sarab and Khuda Afarin, and north of the Aras. Qarabagh, Qaradagh and Shirvan were occupied, but Mishkin, Moghan and Talesh were left in Iranian control and administered from Ardabil.[3] This was now a politically sensitive frontier region, particularly as it contained the Safavid shrines at Ardabil, though it was probably also by 1600 in a state of considerable desolation.

Abbas recovered Azerbaijan in 1603–4 and Shirvan in 1607, and once again peopled the area with loyal tribes, including some at least of those who later came to be known as Shahsevan, the King's Friends; others immigrated to the area during the 17th century. Eastern Azerbaijan ceased to be a frontier region, and enjoyed nearly 100 years of comparative tranquillity. Iran included much of Georgia and Daghistan in the northwest, while Khorasan and large areas of present-day Afghanistan and Pakistan lay within Iran's eastern frontier. Some territory in the west was lost to the Turks in the 1630s, but after the Treaty of Zohab in 1639 the frontier province of Azerbaijan had been so secure from invasion that it had for much of the time been counted as an internal province and ruled directly from the capital.

Spontaneous settlement of both the wealthier and the poorer nomads may well have occurred, especially in Moghan. Here, apart from Timur's canals, which may or may not still have been operating, in 1700 a new canal from the Aras was constructed by order of the local khan; and by 1725 the irrigated lands (*anhār*) of Moghan must have been of some extent, to judge from the revenue assessment recorded that year in the *Tadhkirat al-Mulūk*.[4] A considerable area by the lower Aras and Kor (the Moghan, Shirvan and Qarabagh steppes) was irrigated at least until 1733, but was probably destroyed finally by Nadir Shah a few years later – so says Monteith, who observed the remains of some of these canals in about 1831. Traces of them, somewhat dwarfing late 20th-century irrigation schemes, can still be observed today in Iranian Moghan, as can massive ruins of medieval cities that must have thrived on them. Ironically, Nadir Shah is remembered locally not as their destroyer but as their builder, one large canal being called after him.[5]

After the Safavids

The beginning of the 18th century found Iran in a condition of steadily worsening administrative and military decay under the weak and misguided Shah Sultan Hussain. Long tranquil frontiers were soon to crumble. Internally, ominous signs included revolts in Shirvan and Moghan around the turn of the century.

The death throes of the Safavid dynasty began with the Afghan invasions in the south and east, culminating in 1722 in the siege and capture of Isfahan by Mahmud Ghiljai, while the west and northwest soon fell carrion to the voracious Ottomans and Russians, both newly freed from military commitments elsewhere to expand in the direction of Iran. For several crucial years eastern Azerbaijan formed the crossroads of three empires, and the Shahsevan and other tribal groups of the region were thrust into a political rôle as frontiersmen for which they must have been ill prepared.

In the early 1720s, Ottomans won control of Georgia, Armenia and Shirvan and threatened Azerbaijan, while the Russians occupied the southwest shores of the Caspian (Darband, Baku, Gilan). By the 1724 Russo–Ottoman Treaty, the frontier between them bisected Shirvan and Moghan, leaving Shamakhi to the Turks. From Javat in Moghan, the Turko/Iranian frontier was to run south towards the Safavid shrine-city of Ardabil, which was left to Tahmasp, and then straight on to Hamadan. The Russians were to retain control of the Caspian provinces they had already won, while the Ottomans had still to take possession of their allotted zone. This they did in 1725, but with the death of Peter the Great they moved on to take Ardabil too, forcing Shah Tahmasp, who had taken refuge there, to retreat to Qazvin. Most of the Shahsevan tract, from Moghan to Ardabil, was in the hands of the Ottomans, who appointed governors to their sector of Moghan and to Qaradagh, which then included Mishkin, the home of the Shaqaqi tribes.[6] The Russians had already entrusted their territories in Salyan and Moghan to the authority of Ali Quli Khan Shahsevan, the big landowner in those parts.

Between 1726 and 1728 most of the local tribes, especially the Shahsevan and the Shaqaqi, supported by the Russians, fought guerrilla resistance against the Ottomans, trying especially to drive them from Ardabil. In early 1729 Ottoman forces finally defeated them, receiving the surrender of the Inallu and Afshar Shahsevan and the Shaqaqi of Mishkin, while the other Shahsevan and the Moghanlu tribe took refuge with the Russians near Salyan, becoming Russian subjects.

Only a small sector of the Ottoman/Russian frontier, north of Shamakhi, was ever demarcated. According to Major Gärber, one of the Russian commissars appointed to the frontier demarcation, in 1728 Shahsevan and Moghanlu nomads would come in winter to rent grazing for their flocks in the Salyan district,[7] whose excellent pastures were due to the annual summer flooding in the Kor delta. Their horses were the finest in Iran.

At the end of 1729, the brilliant general Tahmasp Quli Khan Qirqlu Afshar, later called Nadir Shah, disposed of the Ghiljais and restored Safavid rule at Isfahan in the person of Shah Tahmasp. In the following year he managed to recover from the Ottomans all western Iran and most of Azerbaijan, including Ardabil, which was taken with Russian help. Later in the year he was distracted by an Afghan uprising in Khorasan; in his absence from Azerbaijan in 1731, Shah Tahmasp rashly attacked the Ottomans there, and lost most of the newly recovered territory – Ganjeh, Tiflis, Erivan, Nakhchivan, Shirvan and Daghistan – the Ottoman frontier with Iran being fixed at the Aras. However, Nadir returned and retrieved the lost ground, and by the end of 1733 Turkey gave up all claim to the territory that had been seized, and the frontier of the Treaty of Zohab (1639) was resumed. By the Treaty of Rasht in 1732, Russia ceded the Caspian provinces south of the Kor, including Moghan. Ali Quli Khan Shahsevan continued to hold Salyan for the Russians, but the Shahsevan nomads were among the peoples who now returned to Iranian control.

In the winter of 1734–5 Nadir marched through Ardabil to Moghan and Shirvan to defeat the Lazgis. He besieged Ganjeh in November with Russian assistance, and by the Treaty of Ganjeh (February 1735), Baku and Darband were restored to Iran. The Russian army of occupation, having suffered terrible losses in the south Caspian climate, now withdrew. In Salyan, Ali Quli Khan Shahsevan had served the Russians well; he was now recommended to the mercy of Nadir, who took him into his retinue. Those groups that had surrendered to the Ottomans, however, namely the Inallu and Afshar Shahsevan and the Shaqaqi, were among the tens of thousands of tribal families whom Nadir removed to Khorasan. Other groups escaped transportation, slaughter and the ravages and requisitions of Nadir's campaigns by flight beyond the frontiers or into mountain fastnesses.

After a further campaign in the southwestern Caucasus against the Ottomans, culminating in the victory of Baghavard (June 1735), Nadir received the surrender of Ganjeh, Tiflis and Erivan by October. In January 1736 he camped in Moghan near the Javat bridge, where he held his famous *qurultay* assembly of the chiefs, mullahs and nobles of the newly reconquered Iranian empire, and where they duly elected him their ruler. Among those present was Ali Quli Khan Shahsevan's son Badr Khan, who was appointed chief of the Shahsevan by Nadir Shah, and from whom the 19th-century paramount chiefs of the Shahsevan of Moghan and Ardabil are descended.[8]

Badr Khan served Nadir in his Khorasan campaigns, but is not heard of after 1737. In the last years of Nadir's reign, Shirvan and eastern Azerbaijan suffered from his campaigns, depredations and depopulation. Travellers of the time enthused over the rich Moghan pastures, where the royal horses were said to be raised, but noted that they were virtually deserted, as were the nearby villages. It is possible that the Shahsevan too were exiled to Khorasan for a time.

After Nadir Shah's assassination in 1747, Badr Khan's family gained and maintained control of the city of Ardabil and the tribal population of the region, though at some stage the family, the tribes and the territory were split into the Ardabil and Mishkin divisions. Both divisions, through their chiefs, became involved in the complex network of alliance, opposition and intrigue that characterized the khanates of Azerbaijan and the southern Caucasus until the establishment of the Qajars at the end of the century.

The Russian conquest of the southern Caucasus

In early 1796, having reconquered the old Safavid trans-Araxian dependencies of Georgia, Erivan, Qubbeh, Shirvan and Talesh, Agha Muhammad Qajar in his turn was crowned Shah in the plains of Moghan. Later the same year, however, a Russian army sent by Catherine the Great once again appeared in Moghan, though it withdrew on her death that winter.

Following Agha Muhammad's assassination in Qarabagh early in 1797, his nephew Fath 'Ali Shah was until 1803 occupied in dealing with internal opposition, but he maintained his uncle's policy of regarding Georgia and the other Caucasian districts as part of Iran, while fearful of Russian aims there. Tsar Paul annexed Georgia in 1801; when he was assassinated soon after, his successor Alexander I reverted to Catherine's policy of expansion in the Caucasus. In the next two years, unsuccessful attempts were made to negotiate the submission of the khanates of Erivan, Ganjeh and Nakhchivan, all of which had substantial Armenian populations.

In the following two decades, eastern Azerbaijan was swept by two extended wars between the new Qajar rulers of Iran and the Russians, who were expanding south of the Caucasus. The campaigns ceased with the Treaty of Turkmanchai (1828), when the present frontier was established.

The occupation of the Iranian territories of the eastern Caucasus took the Russians from 1804 to 1812. For much of this time Russia was involved in the European war, and so the forces available to the commanders in the Caucasus were greatly inferior in numbers to the Iranian armies that opposed them, and the commanders themselves were often unreliable. The Iranians scored some notable military successes. The Russian troops were, however, better organized, even after the Iranians had benefited from some drilling in the European manner. A brilliant general like Kotlarevski, taking advantage of incompetent enemy leadership, had no difficulty in driving the Iranians south of the River Aras. The war ended with the battle of Aslanduz (1812), fought on the western edge of the Moghan steppe. The peace that followed recognized as Russian territory the greater and better part of the steppe, leaving the Shahsevan nomads, in theory, a choice of becoming Russian citizens or retreating south into Iran.

In October 1813 the Treaty of Gulistan confirmed Shirvan, Qarabagh, Talesh and Moghan as Russian possessions, to the great chagrin of Iran. The Russians, however, were equally disappointed that their frontier was not extended to the Aras in the southwestern Caucasus, where the khanates of Erivan and Nakhchivan remained subject to Iran.[9] The wording of the regulations concerning the frontiers was vague, and the ambiguities were seized on in the ensuing years to justify infringements by both sides, particularly in the region of the Moghan–Talesh hills, and around Lake Gokcha/Sevan in Georgia.

The Iranians had managed to convey a great number of tribespeople across the Aras inside their newly restricted frontiers, but they lost vast areas of valuable grazing lands, notably in the Moghan region. Many contemporary travellers comment, usually from second-hand information, on the Moghan plains. For example, Ker Porter wrote in 1822:

> During the winter and spring months, this immense tract, which is computed at sixty farsangs [350km] in length, and twenty [120km] in breadth, becomes abundant in fertility and the richest pasturage, feeding thousands of flocks belonging to the Eelauts [tribespeople] from the mountains of Azerbijan. It being in the power of the Russian government to shut out these subjects of Persia, from their customary annual fattening on a land now passed to other masters, the recovery of this district cannot but be in the heart of the Shah.[10]

The extent of Moghan is overstated here; but, to judge from my own experience of conditions in Moghan in spring 1966, Kinneir is only slightly exaggerating when he reports: "The Persians say, that the grass is sufficiently high to cover a man and his horse, and hide an army from view, when encamped."[11]

Most of the Shahsevan remained Iranian subjects but, as Porter implies, they were for the moment allowed to continue winter grazing in Moghan, on two conditions: that they continue payment of the pasture-dues (*chobbashi*) to the khan of Talesh, under whose jurisdiction the pastures remained; and that nomadic Russian subjects from Talesh should be permitted to enter Iran in the region of Ujarud during the summer months, as they had done before.

The people of Azerbaijan had suffered particularly from exactions to finance the first war, and with the cholera of the 1820s conditions continued to be desperate. In the northeast of the province, the Shahsevan nomads, straddling a critical frontier and totally dependent on Russian benevolence for permission to use their traditional winter quarters, could not be relied on to support the Iranian armies. As early as 1821 it was reported that some families of Shahsevan had fled to Talesh, pursued across the frontier by Iranian troops, who were rounded up and their commanding officer taken prisoner and sent to Georgia.[12] The Mishkin group at least were already prepared to welcome the Russians should they once more encroach upon Iranian territory. At Ardabil a series of Qajar princes had governed from 1810 onwards, and succeeded in securing regular military levies from the local Shahsevan tribespeople, already semi-settled.

North of the Aras, for a period following the Treaty of Gulistan the khanates of Talesh, Shaki, Shirvan and Qarabagh were restored to their former rulers as Russian puppets. In the years that followed, however, two tendencies built up into the outbreak in 1826 of the second Russo–Iranian war. First, the advent in 1816 of the aggressive Alexis Yermolov as Commander-in-Chief of the Caucasus led to the take-over by Russians of direct local authority, and their pressure on the ambiguous areas of the Iranian frontier. Secondly, the protests of the Iranian religious classes, infuriated by the loss of the Caucasian districts, encouraged the resurgence of military power under Abbas Mirza, and his determination to recover them.

The khanates of the southeastern Caucasus were one by one taken over and their khans deposed: Shaki in 1819, Shirvan in 1820, and Qarabagh in 1822. Only Mir Hasan Khan of Talesh was allowed autonomy by Yermolov, who understood him and his family to be implacably hostile to Iran.[13] Mustafa Khan of Shirvan and Mahdi Quli Khan of Qarabagh fled to Iran, where they were installed near the frontier. They soon began intriguing with supporters in their former capitals, and instigated border infringements by the Shahsevan in Moghan, in retaliation for which Russian troops occupied parts of some Iranian districts such as Ujarud.

> These disputes originate in the licentious conduct of the wandering
> tribes who every winter resort to Moghan and the banks of the Arras,
> for the sake of pasturage. Thefts are mutually committed, which
> brings on retaliation; hostile clans arrange themselves on different
> sides, and scarcely a year passes without some scene of rapine and
> bloodshed.[14]

This tale is one that becomes increasingly familiar as the century proceeds. No doubt the "hostile clans" referred to belonged to the Mishkin and Ardabil divisions of the Shahsevan.

Meanwhile some efforts were being made towards demarcation of the frontier in the southwestern Caucasus; but the commission could not agree on any part of the line that they discussed, and the attempts were abandoned in December 1823. The Russians began encroachments in the Gokcha region, which they eventually occupied in 1825.

Abbas Mirza chose the summer of 1826 to open a full-scale campaign for the recovery of the former Iranian territories in the Caucasus. In addition, once again "one of the principal objects of the war carried on by the Persians against Russia was to induce the Iliyats of Karabagh, Sheki, &c. to return to their allegiance to the Shah".[15] Abbas Mirza's early successes were soon reversed by Yermolov and Paskievitch. The latter led an expedition into Azerbaijan (Qaradagh), followed by another in 1827 by Armenian Prince Madatof to Mishkin. The objectives of these expeditions were twofold: to forage for the troops, and to bring the nomads (or at least their flocks) back north of the Aras.

By late 1827 the Iranians were defeated and Russian forces occupied Tabriz. There was a further expedition, that of Vadibolski to Ardabil, which got stuck in the snow, and Paskievitch's plans to march on Tehran were also frustrated. Ardabil was however occupied in early 1828 by Suchtelen. Peace was signed at Turkmanchai in February, fixing the Azerbaijan frontier with Russia almost exactly as it remains today. The Shah recovered Tabriz and Ardabil and the rest of present-day Iranian Azerbaijan, but renounced any claims to territory north of the Aras and confirmed the loss of Talesh and Moghan.

The aftermath of the wars

Russia's Caucasian frontier with Iran was in many ways as important an arena of the 19th century Great Game as British India's frontier with Afghanistan. Both were of considerable strategic importance, and crossed by major Asian trade routes. The main differences were in the nature of the terrain and the population. While the mountain ranges of the northwest frontier of India were of marginal agricultural value, rugged, remote and defensible, the southern Caucasus included some of the most fertile agricultural lands of the area and for this reason, as well as its comparative accessibility, could not provide so remote and defensible a refuge where tribal populations could remain politically autonomous from competing states and empires.

As Iran was steadily strangled by British and Russian imperial interests, most insidiously by their overt economic penetration of the country, the Shahsevan as frontier tribes suffered not only from the restriction of their grazing lands but also from increasing extortion by the Qajar administration. Not surprisingly they responded by raiding, confined at first to the Russian colonies along and beyond the Kor river. As these depredations spread further afield during the second half of the 19th century, they too became a festering issue between the Russian and Iranian authorities, and were used by both to political advantage.

During the wars, Iranian troops had brought a large number of tribal groups south of the Aras, as described earlier. Some of these groups returned to become Russian subjects, but many remained. Most of the tribes indigenous to Iranian Azerbaijan had co-operated with the Russians during Paskievitch's occupation of the province. Article 15 of the Treaty of Turkmanchai granted them an amnesty and allowed them one year in which, if they chose, to migrate into Russian territory and settle there as Russian subjects. There was indeed considerable movement in a northerly direction: 21 villages in the Talesh, Salyan, Shirvan and Baku districts were completely or partly settled by Shahsevan tribespeople at this time, while certain nomadic groups based in Talesh (and perhaps also the other districts), formerly loosely attached to the Shahsevan confederacy, now chose to take up Russian nationality, though some of them continued to come to Iranian territory during the summer months.[16]

Other nomadic groups left Iranian territory at this time, particularly Kurdish tribes from northwestern Azerbaijan. Fraser, writing of the Iranian authorities' oppression of their subjects in 1833–4, noted that:

> Frequent migrations of the Nomade population take place from the Persian territories into those of Russia; while many of the fixed inhabitants rather long for the hour which shall bestow upon them the fancied protection of the Russian sway.[17]

That a substantial population of nomads and peasants still remained in Ira-

nian Azerbaijan, despite Article 15 of the treaty, and despite official oppression, is probably an indication of the aversion that Muslims felt to the
prospect of subjection to infidel overlords.

For some decades the Shahsevan nomads were permitted limited access
to their traditional winter quarters, as they had been after the Treaty of
Gulistan. In 1828 the Iranian government asked the Caucasian administration to permit the nomads to continue their migrations to Moghan as before,
offering to pay the annual sum of 2000 roubles[18] that had formerly been
paid as pasture-dues to the khans of Talesh. In 1831 a preliminary contract
concerning this was drawn up, specifying conditions by which the nomads'
migrations should proceed and the dues should be paid. The third article
laid down that the Shahsevan tribes should use only that part of the steppe
that had formerly belonged to the Talesh khanate, specifically excluding the
Shirvan part of the steppe. The latter, comprising much of the territory on
the southern banks of the Aras and Kor rivers, was reserved for the use of
Russian nomads and village-based flocks. A copy of the contract was sent
to Tehran for ratification, pending which the Shahsevan were allowed to use
the Moghan pasturage free of charge. But it was not until 1847 that the Iranian government paid the first instalment of the pasture-dues.[19]

Meanwhile Russian colonization of the steppe proceeded. After 1828,
the situation was radically altered and the tsarist government energeti-
cally set about consolidating their territorial gains, the more so since
this coincided with the intensified settlement of nomadic Russian subjects.[20]

From the beginning, however, the new agricultural efforts suffered from raiding by Shahsevan nomads, who destroyed crops, stole animals and plundered
villages. In the course of time, the division of Moghan into the Shirvan and
Talesh sectors lapsed, and the whole territory south of the Kor and Aras was
abandoned to the Shahsevan in the winter. Moreover, some of the Iranian
nomads had been used to crossing the Kor and Aras and wintering on the Mil
(Qarabagh) and Shirvan steppes to the north, and many of them continued
to do so, but they now fell foul of the local nomads for whom these pastures
had been set aside by the Russian authorities, and both there and on the
southern banks of the rivers there was continual bloodshed.[21]

After the end of the wars, as the Russians colonized and settled their new
Transcaucasian territories, they were not interested in the annexation of Iranian Azerbaijan. They put pressure on the Iranians to settle their frontier
tribes, but both sides had much to gain from keeping groups like the Shahsevan nomadic. Iran relied on the nomads' pastoral produce and on their
rôle as frontier guards, while the Russians not only gained considerably
themselves from the Shahsevan contribution to the economy of the Moghan
settlers, but also were able to put to good political use their tally of the latter's complaints of Shahsevan raiding. The officials and diplomats concerned
were well aware of these factors in the situation. The Russians pressed for

settlement of the nomads but knew the Iranians would not be keen, and anyway British representatives advised the Iranians against such a policy. So the Iranian officials took half-measures, succeeding only in lining their pockets and further antagonizing the nomads.

The Iranian government attempted to control the Shahsevan through their chiefs, but the Ardabil branch of the dynasty was now already assimilated into the administration and into urban life, and had lost touch with the tribes, while the Mishkin chiefs either could not or would not restrain the most recalcitrant brigands, and were unacceptable to the Russians. Iranian government policy towards the tribes varied from virtual abdication of authority to predatory expeditions and an attempt in 1860 at wholesale settlement.

Closure of the Moghan frontier

With the Iranian authorities unable or unwilling to exercise more than intermittent control on their frontier, in 1884 the Russians took the planned but inevitable step of closing it to the Shahsevan nomads. The result was economic, social and political upheaval in eastern Azerbaijan. More than two-thirds of the nomads were deprived of their traditional winter pastures and markets. Though efforts were made to find them new ones on the Iranian side of the frontier, inter-tribal disputes grew violent and raiding proliferated. Russian markets had been not only outlets for Shahsevan produce but also sources of various commodities that they needed, particularly agricultural produce and manufactured goods such as firearms and ammunition. After the closure, having little to sell or barter in Moghan, most of the nomads had either to find alternative supplies of such commodities or to settle and farm.

The Azerbaijan administration deliberately hindered this settlement. According to one Russian source, the heir apparent Muhammad Ali did not feel too sure of Russian favour and had alienated the settled population by his oppression, so he turned to cultivating the more powerful nomad tribes and their chiefs as potential military support. The Iranian army had deteriorated ever since irregular tribal levies had been replaced by regular troops early in the century, and was now virtually extinct as a fighting force. The nomad tribes remained the only effective militia, and even they were reliable only when defending their own territory. The old policy, of maintaining a frontier strip of endemic tribal "disorder", was revived as some kind of defence against possible incursions, whether from Kurds and Turks in the west, or from Russians in the north of the province. Not only did the administration oppress the settled population and hinder the nomads from settling, but they even as an instrument of policy encouraged the banditry that was the nomads' only alternative for survival. Mutual raiding of tribe on tribe was used as a means of tax-gathering.[22]

These affairs were reported by Russian officials, who did not, of course, appreciate or admit the degree to which Russian imperialism and the rivalry with Britain in the 19th century were largely responsible for both the frontier closure and the abuses of the Iranian administration. One of them, Markov, concerned only to justify Russian action in closing the frontier and its benefits to the inhabitants of Russian Moghan, did not consider its effects on the Iranian side. Artamonov, however, who visited the region to make a military–geographical study in November 1889, a year after Markov, was shocked at the poverty and oppression of the peasantry and the obvious distress and disorder suffered by the nomads as a result of the closure; his observations were mainly of the Mishkin division of the Shahsevan. Fourteen years later, Tigranov carried out an investigation of the region and published an informative and perceptive account of the economic and social conditions of the Ardabil province and of the nomad and settled Shahsevan tribes, particularly those of the Ardabil division.[23]

For 40 years after the closure the Shahsevan were in almost continual rebellion against all external authority. The chiefs would send raiding parties into Russian territory, sometimes to steal animals and grain from camps and villages, but more often, in the years immediately after the closure, to attack Cossack guard-posts and carry off their firearms, with which the nomads were plentifully supplied by 1900. Throughout these years, the Caucasian administration and the Russian representatives at Tabriz apparently continued to encourage the Shahsevan, supplying them with arms, allowing them to take refuge over the frontier when pursued, and intervening on their behalf when they were captured. Meanwhile they built up their Cossack garrisons at frontier points like Astara and Khuda Afarin, offering their services to the Iranian government, which was able to refuse them only by sending the occasional punitive expeditions. In addition, the Russians took their own reprisals against those of the tribes that raided too flagrantly over the frontier. Their policy was clear: to foster disorder within Iranian territory and to make their own military assistance and eventual occupation indispensable, though they did not achieve this for some years.

Russian military expeditions visited Shahsevan districts for intelligence purposes. Russian merchants and goods dominated the trade of Azerbaijan, and, after Tabriz, Ardabil was the most important commercial centre of the province. Russian subjects were buying many villages in the province, using Iranian proxies in order to overcome legal restrictions. New roads and railways across the province were planned, though a proposed railway south from Aslanduz was rejected as it would run through bandit-infested country. At the beginning of the 20th century, large numbers of Iranians from the Ardabil region used to migrate to Baku to work in the oilfields or the docks for several months of the year; some of them stayed and remitted their earnings to Iran.[24]

In spring 1908, the "Belasovar incident" between tribesmen and Russian guards on the frontier at Deman in Shahsevan territory provided the Russians with a pretext for military intervention in Azerbaijan on a scale that hastened the fall of the Constitutionalist government in Tehran. During the winter of 1908–9, there were some Shahsevan among the reactionary forces that besieged Tabriz, and in late 1909, while the new Nationalist government struggled to establish control of the country, most of the Shahsevan chiefs joined a union of tribes of eastern Azerbaijan, which proclaimed opposition to the constitution and the intention of marching on Tehran and restoring the deposed Muhammad Ali Shah. They plundered Ardabil, receiving wide coverage in the European press. The ex-Shah had however already left for Russia; the union disintegrated, and the tribes were severally defeated by Nationalist forces from Tehran in the early months of 1910. Subsequently the Shahsevan were regarded as dangerous political support for Muhammad Ali's return, while the main activity of their warriors was resistance to the occupying Russian forces.

The actions of the Shahsevan have commonly been dismissed as those of inveterate brigands and implacable anti-constitutionalists. They have had a bad press, both in contemporary newspapers and among historians. European newspapers, particularly (after the 1907 Anglo–Russian agreement) the British, were strongly influenced by the Russians to see the Shahsevan as bandits with "predatory instincts", a "frontier problem" comparable to that of the British on their northwest frontier in India. For example, the *Times* correspondent in St Petersburg, persuaded by the Russians' interpretation of events in Ardabil and their plan for a "final solution", commented:

> The interests of the [Russian] Empire demand a cessation of the anarchy on its borders. A punitive expedition against the Shahsevans would have been undertaken long ago had they indulged their marauding propensities on our Indian border.[25]

For recent historians, Shahsevan involvement in the siege of Tabriz and their sacking of Ardabil have been enough to label them as anti-constitutionalist: thus Cottam, though noting Shahsevan resistance to the Russians as motivated by xenophobia and religious hatred, states that "the Azarbayjani Shahsevan tribe . . . had consistently opposed the Constitutionalists and had been a major source of support for Muhammad 'Ali Shah".[26]

I have elsewhere re-examined the rôle of the Shahsevan at this period, and attempted to explain the reasons for, and to correct, the hostile stereotypes to be found in historical accounts.[27]

In winters after 1916, some of the tribes went back into Russian Moghan, occupied the banks of the Kor and prevented the settlers from irrigating their crops; they were probably partly to blame for the terrible famine suffered in the eastern Caucasus in 1921 and 1922. In September 1918, Russian Azerbaijan was taken over by Turks and Azerbaijanis and declared an independent republic. After the Turks retreated at the end of that year, the first Azerbaijani parliament opened, with support from British forces at Baku.

The British left Baku in August 1919; the Red Army entered and set up a soviet in spring 1920, while many of the largely bourgeois Musavatists, who had dominated the parliament, fled to Iran.

During 1920, Bolshevik forces landed in Gilan and Mazandaran in support of Kuchik Khan and the Jangalis, while their agents were active in Iranian Azerbaijan. Towards the end of the year, with the justifiable excuse that Shahsevan bands were continually encroaching over their frontier and attacking their forces, the Soviet authorities prepared an invasion of Iranian Azerbaijan. One column crossed at Astara in January 1921, only to be heavily defeated. Another column invaded Moghan in the spring and was wiped out by Shahsevan warriors, supported by Musavatist refugees.[28]

In 1923 the Shahsevan were disarmed by Riza Khan (later Riza Shah Pahlavi), and many chiefs were executed or imprisoned. Cross-frontier movements came to an end. A decade later the nomads were forcibly settled, some on the frontier in Moghan, others to the south in Mishkin and elsewhere. Many resumed nomadic migrations by 1941, when Riza Shah was forced to abdicate, and there was a brief revival of chiefly power and tribalism in the 1940s, during the Soviet occupation of Azerbaijan and the short-lived Democratic Republic.

The later Pahlavi period saw growing state control of political and economic affairs, increasing nomad settlement, and a steady decline in the power of chiefs and in the importance of tribal groups for the remaining nomads. Meanwhile, the Russo/Iranian frontier delineated by the Treaty of Turkmanchai has not been significantly altered since, though it was not finally demarcated until 1957.[29] The Iranian government took serious measures to develop the Moghan steppe, by irrigation schemes begun in 1949, and the Aras dam projects developed in the 1960s and 1970s in co-operation with Soviet Azerbaijan.

The Islamic Republic has seen a rehabilitation of pastoral nomadism and of tribal consciousness in eastern Azerbaijan as elsewhere. From the later 1980s, while agricultural and other developments in the Moghan steppe continue, the nomads have enjoyed improvements in infrastructure and other services through the Organization for Tribal Affairs.

Incidents on the Aras frontier in Azerbaijan were among those that inaugurated the breakup of the Soviet Union at the end of the 1980s. A number of diplomatic agreements during 1990 and 1991 considerably improved cross-border access by settlers on either side.[30]

Afterword

Partly by accident and partly by design, Iran's frontiers cut through the territories of a large number of tribal and ethnic communities, separating

34

peoples who are historically and culturally linked. This chapter has traced the history of one frontier sector, that of eastern Azerbaijan, focusing on the rôle of the local nomad tribes, the Shahsevan, and their fortunes as both actors and pawns in the international rivalries that have stormed over them and their territory. The Shahsevan have maintained a strong tradition of identity as guardians of the frontier, a rôle that no doubt they would be ready to play again if future emergencies should demand it.

Notes

1. On royal progresses, see C. Geertz, "Centers, kings and charisma: reflections on the symbolics of power", in his *Local knowledge: further essays in interpretive anthropology* (New York: Basic Books, 1983).
2. The bridge of boats built by Shah 'Abbas was still there in the 18th century.
3. K. M. Röhrborn, *Provinzen und Zentralgewalt Persiens im 16 und 17. Jahrhunderten*, 7 (Berlin: Walter de Gruyter, 1966).
4. V. Minorsky (ed.), *The Tadhkirat al mulūk. A manual of Safavid administration*, 165 (London: Luzac), Gibb Memorial Series NS 16; C. de Bruin, *Travels into Muscovy, Persia and divers parts of the East-Indies*, vol. IV, 12 (London, 1737).
5. J. J. Lerch, "Auszug aus dem Tagebuch von einer Reise . . . ", *Büsching's Magazin* 3 (1769), 18–20; W. Monteith, "Journal of a tour through Azarbdbijan and the shores of the Caspian", *Journal of the Royal Geographic Society* 3 (1833), 30; V. Minorsky, "Mukān", *Encyclopedia of Islam*, 1st edn, 3 (1936), 710–11; V. Minorsky, "Mukān", *Encyclopedia of Islam*, 1st edn, Supplement (1938), 152–3; R. Tapper, "Dašt-e Mogān", *Encyclopedia Iranica* (forthcoming).
6. Küçükçelebizâde Isma'il Asim, *Tarih-i Çelebizâde*, fol. 83b–85b (Constantinople, 1740).
7. The rent was probably payable then, as later, to the Khans of Talesh.
8. This is my interpretation of the evidence; see R. Tapper, *The King's friends: a social and political history of the Shahsevan tribes of Iran* (forthcoming).
9. M. Atkin, *Russia and Iran 1780–1828*, 139–44 (Minneapolis: University of Minnesota Press, 1980).
10. Sir Robert Ker Porter, *Travels in Georgia, Persia, Armenia, Ancient Babylonia, etc., etc. during the years 1817, 1818, 1819 and 1820*, vol. II: 512–13 (London,1821–2).
11. J. M. Kinneir, *A geographical memoir of the Persian empire*, 153 (London, 1813).
12. India Office Library [IOL], "Papers relative to the war between Persia and Russia in 1826, 1827 and 1828", in L/P&S/20,A7 I: 8, no. 12 of 10 February 1821.
13. In fact Mir Hasan threw the Russians out in the year that hostilities reopened, and a strong Iranian force came to help him. He retained control of the khanate, in the name of the Shah, until he was forced to abandon it in 1828 by the Treaty of Turkmanchai.
14. IOL, "Papers relative to the war", I: 8, no. 14 of 10 May 1823.
15. J. Morier, "Some account of the íliyáts, or wandering tribes of Persia . . . ", *Journal of the Royal Geographical Society* 7 (1837), 241.
16. N. von Seidlitz, "Etnograficheskiy ocherk Bakinskoy gubernii", *Kavkazskiy Kalendar na 1871 god* 2 (1870), 1–67; cf. D. I. Ismail-zade, "Iz istorii kochevogo khozyaystva Azerbaydzhana pervoy polovini XIX V", *Istoricheskiy zapiski* (1960), 96–136.
17. J. B. Fraser, *A winter's journey from Constantinople to Tehran*, vol. II: 404 (London, 1838).
18. Some 700 tomans, or £350 at exchange rates of the time.

19. V. Markov, "Shakhseveni na Mugani, Istoriko-etnograficheskiy ocherk", *Zapiski Kavkazskago otdela Imperatorskogo Russkago geograficheskago obshchestva* **19** (1890), 23.

20. F. B. Rostopchin, "Zametki o Shahsevenakh", *Sovetskaya Etnografiya* **3–4** (1933), 98.

21. On nomads in Russian territory at this time, see Ismail-zade, op. cit., also V. P. Kobychev, "Krestyanskoe zhilishche narodov Azerbaydzhana V XIX V", *Kavkazski Etnografischeski Sbornik* **3**, Trudi Instituta Etnografii 79 (Moscow: Akademiya Nauk SSSR, 1962).

22. See passage from Maslovskiy, "Materiali sovrannye iri shtabe Ardebilskogo otryada. Zamyetka o Shahsevenakh", *Izv. Shtaba Kavk. voyennogo okr.* **37** (1914), 7, quoted by Rostopchin, op. cit., 103–4; also Markov, op. cit., 30–2.

23. Markov, op. cit.; L. N. Artamonov, *Severniy Azerbaydzhan. Voyenno-geogr. ocherk.* (Tiflis, 1890); L. F. Tigranov, *Iz Obshchestvenno-ekonomicheskikh otnosheniy v Persii* (St Petersburg, 1909).

24. H. Arfa, *Under five shahs*, 41 (London: John Murray, 1964). In the 1960s I met elderly Shahsevan men who said they had worked in the new cotton plantations in Russian Moghan and Qarabagh.

25. *The Times*, 7 November 1909.

26. R. W. Cottam, *Nationalism in Iran*, 56–7 (Pittsburgh: Pittsburgh University Press, 1964).

27. R. Tapper, "Raiding, reaction and rivalry: Shahsevan tribes in the constitutional period", *Bulletin of SOAS* **49** (1986), 508–31; and "History and identity among the Shahsevan", *Iranian Studies* **21** (1988), 84–108.

28. R. Tapper, "Black sheep, white sheep and red-heads: a historical sketch of the Shahsevan of Azarbaijan", *Iran* **4** (1966), 61–84.

29. See M. Ganji, Chapter 4; A. Jahanbani, *Marz-hā-yi Irān va Shūravi* (Tehran: Ibn Sina, 1957/1336).

30. Information from Abbas Maleki.

CHAPTER FOUR
The historical development of the boundaries of Azerbaijan

M. H. GANJI

Introduction

Delimitation and, to a certain extent, demarcation of Iran's international boundaries date back to the early years of the 19th century. This was the time when frontier-consciousness was awakened in Iran as a result of the impact of the fateful Napoleonic wars in Europe and early contacts between Iran and the West. Before then, frontiers were vaguely based on the extent of sovereignty of the central government over the vassals of the border areas and the authority of the latter over their domains. Traditionally, such vassals were entrusted with the responsibility for guarding the frontiers against neighbouring countries.

The history of the frontiers of Azerbaijan is the story of the interplay between aggression, domination and intimidation on the part of Russia, and weakness, timidity and submission on the part of Iran (Fig. 4.1). This situation has resulted in the attachment of a certain taboo to the question of frontiers. Little has been discussed, less has been written and scarcely any proper research has been done. It is therefore hoped that this chapter will open the way for due attention to be paid to this question and for valuable research to be undertaken in future.

Historical background

At the beginning of the 15th century, or at the dawn of the age of geographical discoveries that were destined to alter the map of the then known world, it appears that Iran's age-old rôle as an intermediary in cultural and commercial relations between East and West had developed in such a way that these relations were carried out along three main routes, as follows:

Figure 4.1 Iran's territorial losses during the reign of Fath 'Ali Shah, 1813–1828.

(a) Tabriz—Erzerum—Sivas—Iskenderun (east Mediterranean coast).
(b) Tabriz—Khoy—Erzerum—Trabzon (east Black Sea coast).
(c) North Iranian cities (Tabriz, Ardabil, Rasht, etc.) over the Caspian Sea to Astrakhan, Moscow and beyond.

It was along the above channels that silk, precious stones, spices and other valuable products of the East found their way to southern and northern European countries. As time went on, and the expanding Ottoman empire extended its power into the heart of Europe, the first two routes, being under Muslim control, became too hazardous for Christian merchants and travellers, which diverted the traffic along, and brought prosperity, to the third route, namely the trade route through the Caspian Sea and its coasts, Moscow and beyond.

Throughout the 16th century many European rulers ventured to establish relations with the Safavid kings of Iran, not only to draw benefit from the promising commercial possibilities, but also to secure an ally against the mighty common enemy, the Ottoman empire. Among the many emissaries, there are records of a certain Englishman by the name of Anthony Jenkinson who travelled in 1561 to the court of the Safavid king Shah Tahmasp I as a delegate of Queen Elizabeth and the Tsar of Russia, Ivan the Terrible.

Although Jenkinson's mission had limited success, it nevertheless marks the first joint effort of England and Russia to establish commercial and diplomatic relations with Iran, which was at that time a strong power controlling the whole of the area south of the Caspian as far as the Persian Gulf. However, Russia, being closer to Iran, gradually encroached upon Iranian territories, taking possession of Kazan and Astrakhan, key points on the route connecting the northern Iranian cities with Moscow.

Meanwhile, in Iran, Shah Abbas the Great was very eager to establish commercial relations with other countries and, in pursuit of this policy, he received with favour a Russian prince who was commissioned by Moscow to conclude a trade agreement that enabled Russian merchants to move freely in Iran and to conduct business under the special protection of the Shah.

The first official trade agreement between the two countries was finalized in 1618, but it was not until the time of Peter the Great of Russia that the relations thus established assumed political aspects. In 1715 Peter commissioned Artemii Volynskii to travel to the Safavid court at Isfahan for the purpose of strengthening the relations already established. This mission coincided with events in Iran that resulted in the downfall of the Safavids and the temporary ascendency of the Afghan rulers. Volynskii observed the chaotic state of affairs in Iran and reported to his master that there could be no better opportunity for Russia to attack Iran and take possession of the coveted lands that would make possible Russian access to the warm southern waters. Peter realized that this long-cherished ambition was within his grasp, and in 1722 himself led an army that captured Astrakhan at the strategic head of the Volga. He then proceeded to Darband, where he established a garrison before returning to his capital. He nevertheless showed a friendly gesture to the last Safavid Shah, Sultan Hussain, instructing his envoy to offer assistance in overcoming the Afghan rebels. On the way to Isfahan, this envoy met the crown prince Tahmasp Mirza in Qazvin and persuaded him to send an emissary to Moscow and, as the rightful heir to the throne of Iran, formally to ask for assistance as suggested. Tahmasp, being quite destitute and reckless, accepted the offer and sent a close relative, Isma'il Beg, to Moscow. Peter then showed his intentions by informing Tahmasp's envoy that he would send an army to save the Safavid throne on condition that:

(a) the two cities of Darband and Badkuba (present Baku) were formally ceded to Russia;

(b) the two provinces of Mazandaran and Asterabad were allocated to Russia in order to supply food and provisions for the ceded cities.

The Iranian envoy accepted these shameful conditions and signed the agreement of September 1723 generally known as the St Petersburg Treaty, which is regarded as the first official Russian aggression on Iranian territory. The crown prince, however, refused to honour this agreement, and punished his envoy most severely for having signed such a derogatory document.

Soon after conclusion of the St Petersburg agreement, the Russian armies penetrated the provinces of Mazandaran and Asterabad on the pretence of stopping the Afghans from occupying them.

It is of interest to note that, parallel with these developments, the Ottoman empire took the opportunity offered by the chaotic state of affairs in Iran and, apparently with the agreement of the Russian empire, occupied most of the western provinces of Iran, including Erivan, Tabriz, Maragheh, Hamadan and Kermanshah. Later on, however, on becoming aware of the St Petersburg agreement and the Russian penetration of the northern provinces of Iran, the Ottomans strongly protested to Moscow and even threatened to break off relations with Russia. At this stage the French ambassador intervened and consequently the two empires (Russia and the Ottoman empire) came to an agreement whereby each of the two parties became definite possessor of the part of Iranian territory that was at the time under its control. According to this agreement, brought about through French intervention, all Iranian territories lying to the east of the Aras–Kor junction as far as Asterabad were recognized as Russia's share of the booty, while all the land lying to the south of the above junction, as far as Kermanshah, went to the Ottoman empire. The agreement in question, concluded in June 1724, marks the greatest territorial revision officially recorded up to that time.

Fortunately for Iran this adverse agreement was soon to be nullified when a strong leader and warrior, namely Nadir Shah Afshar, came to power. Nadir Shah embarked on a brilliant career in which he first consolidated his power locally, then recovered all the territories lost after the fall of the Safavids, and finally conquered India. In his relations with Russia, Nadir Shah first acted very wisely and amicably by sending an envoy, with valuable presents, to the court of Peter's successor, Empress Anna Ivanovna. At the same time he asked for the return of all territories taken over by her predecessor, failing which he would side with Russia's Ottoman enemies.

Realizing that Nadir was not the kind of Iranian royalty to be ignored and, being inclined to secure a strong neighbour as a counter-balance to the Ottoman empire, the empress received Nadir Shah's envoy with due respect and, in the mean time, agreed to return all the territories unconditionally. Furthermore, as a gesture of good neighbourly relations, she sent a very high-ranking prince as her envoy to the court of Nadir Shah, who was at the time in Ganjeh awaiting developments. It was in that city that the treaty known as the Treaty of Ganjeh was exchanged in 1735. This event was of particular importance and is of great interest because by its terms the River Sulagh was officially recognized as the international frontier between Russia and Iran. It is of further importance because it is probably the only occasion in relations between the two countries on which Russia agreed to withdraw to its previous frontiers. In response to the Empress's friendly attitude in returning the Iranian territories, Nadir Shah, upon returning from his triumphant march to India, while informing her of his victories, sent her a present of no fewer than 14 Indian elephants.

Nadir Shah was assassinated in 1747, after which Iran was torn by internal struggles for power among tribal chieftains and local vassals. The chaotic conditions went on for almost 40 years, during which period, fortunately for Iran, both Russia and the Ottoman empire had their own preoccupations in Europe, with the result that they had little opportunity to pay attention to their border problems with Iran. However, one incident of this period is worthy of attention because it involved frontier and territorial changes. In 1783, the former vassal Erekle of Georgia revolted against the central government of Iran and sought help from the Empress of Russia, Catherine. She accepted his plea for the protection of his Christian subjects from Islamic aggression and despatched armies for his support. After some encounters, the Iranian forces were defeated and an agreement was concluded in the same year (1783) under which Georgia was virtually separated from Iran and came under Russian domination.

The Qajar dynasty and the Russo–Iranian wars

The rivalry over power among local vassals and tribal chieftains resulting from the assassination of Nadir Shah came to an end when Agha Muhammad Khan, the founder of the Qajar dynasty, proclaimed himself Shah of Iran. This strong eunuch king spent the first years of his rule consolidating his power and bringing all local governors under his command. He then aimed at chastising the vassal of Georgia, who had caused the separation of that province from Iran. He personally led an army that captured and sacked Tiflis (Tbilisi), capital of Georgia, in 1795. He thus brought Georgia and the neighbouring areas under his command. By so doing, Agha Muhammad Khan restored the international boundary between his kingdom and Russia to its previous conditions. However, the following year the Empress Catherine of Russia retaliated by sending Russian forces not only to recover Georgia but to advance as far south as the Moghan steppes. At that point the Empress died, and subsequently in 1797, the Qajar monarch once again led his army towards Transcaucasia. It was on the occasion of this fateful expedition that he too met his death at the hands of two of his close guards. Georgia thus remained under Russian rule and the international boundary was pushed south so as to exclude the whole of Georgia from Iranian domains.

The aggression thus begun by Russia did not stop in later years. During the reign of Fath 'Ali Shah, the second Qajar king, Russian armies advanced south as far as Erivan, the capital of Armenia. They then embarked on a policy of maltreating the Muslim inhabitants of the occupied provinces. To give an example of maltreatment on the part of Russia, the following account, although relating to the eastern boundary area, may be quoted here:

> The Russians from time immemorial had not only insisted that all the water of frontier rivers should be devoted to irrigating the cotton fields of Turkestan, but had gone so far as to compel the Persians inhabiting the frontier regions to root up all their trees so that no part of the water should be absorbed in Persian territory. As a consequence considerable districts formerly fertile had been reduced to an arid state. (Public Record Office, Persia, 1947: 51)

Their treatment of the Muslim inhabitants of the occupied provinces in Transcaucasia was no better, and this was indeed one of the factors that caused the fateful Russo–Iranian wars of the early 19th century.

It must be pointed out at this stage that, in the early years of the 19th century, Iran had become the coveted land and a target for the rivalry of the three European powers, namely Great Britain, France and Russia, as well as the Ottoman empire. This was because, by that time, all these countries had realized the tremendous strategic importance of Iran in connection with the resources and riches of India. It was in these circumstances that the first Russo–Iranian war started. During the war years, Fath 'Ali Shah first sought French assistance, and his mission signed a treaty of alliance with Napoleon in Finkelstein (East Prussia) in 1807. Consequently a strong body of military advisers arrived in Tehran to train Iranian officers for fighting the Russians. They were headed by General Gardanne, a well known figure in the history of Iran. Napoleon's aim was to use Iran as an ally in the invasion that he had planned to undertake against India with the help of the Russians, whereas Fath 'Ali Shah was interested only in the recovery of his lost territories. In the mean time, Napoleon had signed the Treaty of Tilsit, a disappointment to the Shah of Iran, who then turned to the British for assistance. However, since relations between France and Russia had deteriorated, the British persuaded the Shah to accept a reconciliation with Russia, thus using their influence in favour of the latter. Consequently Fath 'Ali Shah reluctantly submitted, and came to terms with his enemy. The result of this interference by the British was the well known Treaty of Gulistan, signed between Iran and Russia on 12 October 1813. The key point in this treaty was that the parties concerned should take final possession of all the territories that each of them had under its control at the time of signing the treaty. As a result of this imposed treaty, Iran lost extensive territories including the provinces of Georgia, Darband, Baku, Shirvan, Shaki, Ganjeh, Moghan and even part of Talesh, which were all under Russian control at the time the treaty was signed. The international boundary was fixed vaguely by a line connecting Ghezil Aghaj Bay on the Caspian to Batum on the Black Sea coast.

The Treaty of Gulistan brought a 10-year war to an end, but the hostilities between Iran and Russia did not cease and the frontier disputes remained unsolved for years to come. Throughout the years following the Treaty of

Gulistan, Russia continued to advance further south, and in 1825 claimed the district of Gokcha. This claim was dismissed by the government of Iran. Consequently the second Russo–Iranian war began in 1826. The Iranian armies fought brilliantly in the early phases but were eventually defeated by the stronger and better-equipped Russian army headed by the well known General Paskievitch, who was later able to capture Erivan and Tabriz. This time, too, Iran was persuaded by the British to submit to another damaging treaty: that of Turkmanchai concluded in February 1828. Under its terms, the provinces of Erivan (the whole of present Armenia), Nakhchivan, Qarabagh and parts of Moghan were finally separated from Iran.

The international frontier between Iran and Russia in Azerbaijan was established by Article 4 of the Turkmanchai Treaty, more or less as it stands today, with the River Aras (Araxes) forming most of the frontier, and with a small deviation to the south of its mouth so as to bring Lankoran and its environs under Russian control.

The international boundary, as determined by Article 4, was defined very vaguely, but the treaty had envisaged a joint commission to demarcate the frontier in due course. This commission was soon formed and a protocol was signed in 1829. The protocol, prepared in great haste, detailed only very salient features of the terrain such as prominent peaks, river courses, etc., and made no reference to villages, pastures, or islands within or around the Aras river. Consequently, the Russians gradually encroached on many settlements and forced the inhabitants, by maltreatment, to abandon their homes and to seek refuge across the border. Hundreds of families thus saved their lives and escaped to Iran. There are at present in Iran thousands of the descendants of such refugees whose names indicate their Caucasian origin and who have made notable contributions to later developments in Iran.

The encroachment of Russia on Iranian territories, mostly caused by the inadequate definition of the borderline in the 1829 protocol, went on for almost a century. During this long period many joint commissions were formed to finalize the actual demarcation of the international frontier, but no agreement could be reached because the Russians did not accept the terms of the Turkmanchai Treaty and the 1829 protocol. Disputes always arose from the fact that members of the joint commissions would not accept the responsibility of pinpointing the vaguely defined spots on the ground or on the maps at their disposal.

The 1907 Anglo–Russian agreement, dividing Iran into two spheres of interest, pushed aside all frontier disputes for some time, since the Russian side to the agreement practically ignored all international codes of conduct and in 1910 occupied Tabriz and Mashad, where they put hundreds of innocent inhabitants to death. During the First World War, in spite of the fact that Iran had declared its neutrality, Russian armies occupied parts of Azerbaijan without any regard to international frontiers.

Russo/Iranian frontier disputes after the Russian revolution

After the revolution of 1917 in Russia, drastic changes occurred in that country's relations with its neighbours. As far as Iran was concerned, the major change was embodied in the friendly agreement of 1921 concluded between the two countries. In this treaty the newly created Soviet government waived many concessions that had been unjustly obtained from Iran by the former Tsarist empire.

The question of international frontiers was dealt with in Article 3 of the 1921 agreement. This article placed on record the willingness of the two parties to solve their frontier disputes in a friendly manner. The 1829 protocol was to be the basis of demarcation, and a joint commission was to be created to accomplish the actual demarcation.

As indicated before, most of the frontier disputes arose from the fact that the representatives of the two countries could not agree on the definitions and pinpointing of the localities on the maps and on the ground. As far as the frontiers of Azerbaijan were concerned, disputes centred around areas on the banks of, and islands within, the Aras river on the one hand, and the Moghan steppes on the other.

After the conclusion of the 1921 agreement, no fewer than five joint commissions were formed:
- Mansour–Hakimoff in 1923
- Elhami–Lazaroff in 1925
- Alam–Maevsky in 1951
- Sayyah–Lavrentioff in 1954
- Jahanbani–Orloff in 1955.

Each of the first three commissions achieved some progress in discussing points of dispute along the entire Russo/Iranian frontier, on both sides of the Caspian Sea, but none arrived at a final conclusion. This was mainly because, in almost all cases, the Russian delegates openly insisted that all points of dispute should be definitely ceded to them, to which the Iranians could not agree.

The fourth commission, namely that of Sayyah and Lavrentioff, was on the whole more successful in coming to some conclusive results that led to the actual signing of an agreement in which the formation of another joint commission for the demarcation of the borderline, as defined in this agreement, was envisaged. This last commission was the most effective of all those formed since 1829. It began its work in January 1955 and continued without interruption until it finished the job in 1957. The Iranian side was headed by General Amanollah Jahanbani, one of the most well educated and experienced officers of the Iranian army. He had seen his initial military training in the Military Academy of the Tsarist empire in Moscow, and was therefore thoroughly familiar with the Russian language as well as with the culture and customs of that country. The head of the Russian side was Paul

Dimitrievich Orloff, himself an ambassador of wide experience and good will.

The main functions of the 1955 Jahanbani–Orloff joint commission were to implement the resolutions adopted by the Sayyah–Lavrentioff commission of the previous year. The latter had already agreed broadly on the borderline all along the frontier between the two countries, that is to say, on both sides of the Caspian Sea.

Before starting the actual demarcation, the two parties had agreed that:

(a) accurate maps, to the scale of 1:10,000, be prepared of a 2 km wide strip of land all along the frontier, 1 km into the territory of each side;

(b) the final borderline be defined by a line of strong wooden poles, with two other lines, each at a distance of 2.5 m from the central line, on which permanent concrete pillars were to be erected, numbered and painted with each country's official colour;

(c) accurate co-ordinates for all points within this strip should be calculated and carefully listed in special books;

(d) although the 1929 protocol and the 1954 agreement were to be the main bases for the demarcation of the borderline, all alterations of the past century were to be discussed and all existing pertinent documents were to be studied until all disputes were settled with the consent of both parties.

The joint commission selected Astara as its headquarters, each group being settled in its respective part of that town. Ten subcommittees were appointed, each equipped with appropriate surveying facilities and manned by expert technicians and interpreters.

Demarcation began on the westernmost point of the frontier, at a point on the junction of the Iranian–Turkish–Russian territories as fixed in 1925, and ended at a point specified by pillar no. 144 on the Caspian coast near the mouth of the Astara river, halfway between Iranian Astara and Russian Astara.

The total length of the frontier was determined as 796.5 km, along which 144 main and 305 subsidiary pillars were erected. Wherever rivers were involved, efforts were made to determine and demarcate the median line. In the course of this demarcation there turned out to be no fewer than 805 islands of varying sizes within the actual channel of the River Aras. Of these, 427 islands belonged to Iran and the remaining 378 belonged to Russia. Two of the larger islands were divided between the countries.

Briefly speaking, of the 796.5 km frontier between Iran and Russia to the west of the Caspian Sea, some 475 km coincide with the course of the River Aras between Dim-Ghishlagh in the west and Tazehkand in Moghan in the east. The remainder consists of land frontiers between Tazehkand and the mouth of the Astara river.

The final protocol, along with piles of maps, minutes of meetings, records of surveys, books of co-ordinates, etc., all prepared in Farsi and Russian, was exchanged in Tehran on 11 April 1957, a date that marks the end of century-old frontier disputes on the Azerbaijan borders of Iran.

Eight years after completion of the frontier demarcation as outlined above, the two countries embarked on the implementation of a new venture: the building of a dam on the River Aras. This dam was completed in 1970, but necessitated a new demarcation of the frontier along the lake created behind the new dam and by some changes brought about in the course of the river. A new joint commission was set up to mark the new frontier. This commission worked along the 64.59 km of the border lying between the signs 7–2 and 18. A number of signs and pillars were replaced by new ones on both sides of the lake. The actual new frontier line was fixed by means of permanent buoys along the lake.

Finally, a new protocol was drawn up as an annexe to the agreement dated 2 December 1954 relating to frontier disputes. This protocol, the last on Russo/Iranian frontiers in Azerbaijan, was signed in Moscow on 7 May 1970.

Bibliography

Persian sources

Iranian Ministry of Foreign Affairs, Archival materials in Persian.

Iranian Ministry of Energy. 1990. *Energy, water resources atlas of Iran*, vol. 2: *Hydrology*. Tehran: Ministry of Energy.

Jahanbani, A. 1957. *Frontiers of Iran and Soviet Russia*. Tehran: Ibn-Sina.

Mokhber, M. A. 1947. *Frontiers of Iran*. Tehran: Keyhan.

Other sources

Public Record Office. 1947. Persia, Confidential print no. 917188. Section I: Persian frontiers. E1011, 31 January 1947, 51.

Watson, H. S. 1967. *Russian Empire, 1801–1917*. Oxford: Oxford University Press.

CHAPTER FIVE

The question of Kurdistan and Iran's international borders

MARIA T. O'SHEA

Whither Kurdistan?

Apart from being the name of one of Iran's 25 provinces, Kurdistan exists largely as a cultural, and increasingly political, abstract. It exists as a region within the hearts and minds of the majority of Kurds, and their sympathizers, yet this region is unlikely to be found on any academic maps, and will certainly not be found on any maps produced by the government agencies of the four countries that Kurdistan overlaps. Kurdistan's existence as a discrete area containing a fairly homogeneous population of Kurdish-speaking Indo-Europeans, cannot be doubted. Indeed such an area has been recognized, documented and mapped by outsiders for over 100 years.[1] The *Sharafnameh*, an epic history of the Kurdish people between 1290 and 1596, written by Sharaf Khan Bitlisi in 1596, probably contained the first indigenous attempt at defining the limits of Kurdistan.[2] Since the 1940s, attempts have also been made by certain Kurds themselves to map the region, culminating in the adoption of a stylised map of Greater Kurdistan. This map has become almost an inalienable part of the Kurdish nationalist mythology, to the extent that many Kurds seriously believe that the area traditionally inhabited by Kurds reaches to one or more seas, giving essentially landlocked Kurdistan port cities.[3] It is this question of the extent of the area that can be defined as Kurdistan and of its exact borders that is probably the most vexing even for Kurds. Kurds share, since the time of the venerable Sharaf Khan, a predilection for exaggerating their numbers and their area of habitation, both historically and in the present time. Their host countries, currently Iran, Iraq, Syria and Turkey, similarly share a predilection for underestimating and even falsifying the Kurds' numbers and habitat. All of these states have at various times made their own attempts at reducing the Kurdish population, either absolutely or just within the zone of Kurdistan itself.

It is not within the scope of this chapter to elaborate further on the topic of Greater Kurdistan, other than to point out that Kurdistan undoubtedly exists as a "social and political concept",[4] and its perception is a contentious

47

issue between the Kurds and their host states and indeed amongst the Kurds themselves. This region straddles two of Iran's international boundaries and thus it is interesting to examine how its existence, or even its official non-existence, has affected the development and maintenance of Iran's western boundary within Kurdistan. It is my contention that Kurdistan or the Zagros axis has functioned as a border region, with few interruptions for millennia, both because of its rôle as a natural mountain barrier in an area of successive empire expansion, and more recently because of its ethnic and religious composition. The existing international boundary of western Iran is very similar to the boundary between the Ottoman and Persian empires

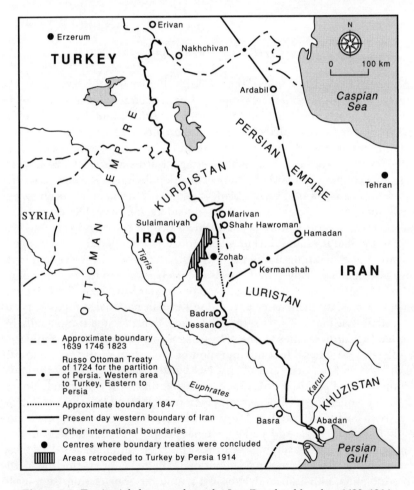

Figure 5.1 Territorial changes along the Iran/Iraq land border, 1639–1914.

48

in existence since the 17th century (Fig. 5.1). However, it has been only really in the 20th century that the existence of such a boundary has made itself felt in the lives of the region's inhabitants. It would seem that existing as a border region was a far more profitable and comfortable state of affairs than living in a region bisected or even trisected by enforced international boundaries, which is the situation in which the Kurds find themselves. The resilience of this boundary, despite many compelling reasons to challenge it and the vicissitudes that have befallen the area, is surprising, and may imply that the location offers certain advantages that are not immediately apparent.

The historical antecedents

The Anatolia–Zagros axis has formed a natural barrier to empire expansion since Sargon (2371–16 BC) and his successors created the first Mesopotamian empire. Sargon's empire collapsed partly as a result of repeated raids by mountain dwellers from the central Zagros. The successive empires of Ur, Assyria and Babylon also failed to breach the Zagros divide. The Zagros region was home to many small kingdoms and city-states, mostly known of only through the records of the contiguous plains cultures. In the 3rd millennium BC the Qutils established a unified kingdom and were the only Zagros group to conquer part of Mesopotamia, namely Akkadia and Sumeria, which they ruled from 2250 to 2120 BC. The constant friction between the plains and mountain dwellers so weakened the Zagros tribes that the Medes and other Aryan invaders found little resistance. The Median empire was based in the heart of the Zagros range – for the first time an empire straddled this region, and for the last time the mountain people were able to dominate the plains dwellers.[5] Although technically the whole region was under Persian control by the 6th century BC, there is little evidence that the central government was able to exert any real control over these mountains, which were after all just a staging post on the way to the rest of the empire. At the start of the Persian–Greek rivalry, Xenophon noted in 401 BC that the Karduchoi who lived in the Zagros mountains were fully independent and paid no homage to the Persian ruler.[6] The Greek historian Diodorus, adds that the inhabitants of these mountains were so much trouble to the empires and foreign armies that efforts were directed solely at dissuading them from raiding the plains.[7]

Around the time of the decline of the Hellenistic empire, most of the Zagros rulers either joined the Parthian federation or were absorbed by it. During the four centuries of the Parthian era (247 BC to AD 226) there were seven semi or fully independent principalities around the area that would later correspond to the western Iranian borders. These were (with their corresponding present regions): Mada (Media); Elymais (Luristan); Kerm (Kermanshah); Mukriyan (Mahbad); Shahrezur (Sulaimaniyah), Barchan (Barzan); and Sanak (Sahna).[8] Even the following Sassanian empire was unable to exert direct control over this region, and was forced to resort to the use of vassal kings until the strong centralization drive of Ardeshir II.

Religion enters as a factor

The invading Arab Islamic armies defeated the Persian Sassanid empire, commencing with the Battle of Qadissiah in AD 642, and concluding with a final decisive battle at Nehevand, significantly within this strategic Zagros axis, ushering in a period of relative calm for the region, the Islamic empire's frontier being far away to the north with the Byzantine empire in Anatolia. The inhabitants of the Zagros were converted to Islam only fitfully, and never entirely. The region was to remain a religious as well as ethnic mosaic well into the 20th century. The Armenian population remained resolutely Christian, as did many Kurds and those people believing themselves to be the remains of the Assyrian population; a substantial Jewish population existed amongst the Kurds until the 1950s; several neo-Zoroastrian groups remain until the present day and the Kurdish inhabitants' acceptance of Islam was selective, resulting in the practice of several syncretic versions of Islam. Other religious groups adopted some outward manifestations of Islam in order to avoid persecution, yet continued ancient practices.[9]

Persia initially produced a great number of the major contributors to Islamic thought, as well as Islam's first mystics. The Zagros region produced no major Islamic figures, but the muslim Kurds of the region adopted the Shafai school of Islam, at least superficially, as initially practised in Persia. However, the incomplete absorbtion of Persia into the Arab Islamic empire was a factor in the Sunni/Shi'a schism at the end of the 7th century. Persians, chafing under Arab cultural and political domination, sought a way to re-establish their past cultural and political heritage and to halt the encroachment of Arabism in Persia. The majority of Persian thinkers resented the superiority of the Arabs and the perceived theft of their achievements by the less socially advanced Arabs. By the 14th century, Persia finally adopted Shi'ism as the state religion under Shah Ismail I (1502–18), the first Safavid Shah. This meant that the Zagros region became not only the buffer between the Arab, and later Ottoman, culture and the Persian culture but a buffer between the two major branches of Islam.

The majority of the largely Kurdish inhabitants of western Persia remained Sunni, as they had little contact with Persian culture, and thus had little empathy with the Persians' feelings of humiliation and resentment of domination by a "lesser" culture. Those Kurds who were Moslems were in fact more likely to identify with the Caliph, initially Arab and later Ottoman. Along with the Kurds outside the area of Persian control, they remained indifferent to the proselytizing attempts of the Safavids.

Kurdistan – province, principality and pawn

The first known use of the name Kurdistan dates from the time of the last great Seljuk Sultan of Persia, Sultan Sandjar (d.1157), who created the first Kurdish administrative province. This province, to the northwest of Hamadan, with its capital at Bahar, encompassed the whole of the area between Azerbaijan and Luristan, and included the regions of Hamadan, Dinawar, Kermanshah and Sennah (Sanandaj) to the east of the Zagros mountains and to the west of Shahrezur and Khuftiyan, on the Zab river.[10] This area, straddling the present-day border between Iran and Iraq, was to be the largest state-acknowledged area to be known as Kurdistan, and fluctuated both in its extent and degree of freedom from central government control. Kurdistan's time as merely the periphery of empire was to last for around 300 years. During this time, the inhabitants were largely at the service of whichever empire might require their services and skills, mainly of a martial nature.

Kurdistan was to become the main theatre for Ottoman–Persian rivalry, destroying any hopes for continuing Kurdish unity. Mesopotamia and the area to the north were to be the target of rivalry between the newly emergent Shia Safavid Persian empire and the Sunni Ottoman Turkish empire, which perceived Persia's religious heresy as much a challenge to its legitimacy as its competing territorial claims. The Persian capture of Baghdad in 1508 was reversed at the Battle of Calderan in 1514. Kurdish military aid to the Ottoman Sultan Selim the Cruel won them a pact that formally recognized 16 Kurdish principalities of various sizes and about 50 Kurdish *sanjaks* (fiefdoms) within the Ottoman empire. These principalities were totally sovereign, although bounden not to rise against the Sultan or to alter their frontiers. Thus, even at a time of recognition of Kurdish sovereignty, the spectre of a united Kurdistan guided any negotiations on the part of the Ottomans. Calderan marked the beginning of a successful policy of pitting the Kurdish principalities and tribes against both the rival empire and each other to prevent a unified region. Mesopotamia was lost and won twice more in the next 30 years, each time with the aid of Kurdish mercenaries. Although the Kurds generally sided with the Ottomans as co-religionists, they were frequently receptive to inducements from the Persians. The Kurdish principalities and tribes became most adept at exploiting their situation.

The rival empires came to realize that they had little to gain from this tug-of-war, except maybe financial ruin, so they concluded the Treaty of Amasya in 1555. This first attempt at a political solution to the regional conflict was to last for only 20 years. Further fighting led to the Persians re-conquering Mesopotamia in 1623, only to cede it to the Ottomans again in 1638. The following year saw the Treaty of Zohab, and the first mutual acceptance of a broad border swathe between the two empires. The border was based on the existing tribal loyalties within the region, but owing to the shifting nature of these loyalties the frontier zone was over 160 kilometres wide from the Zagros in the east to the Tigris in the west. The imperial conflict was now contained within this zone. Thus the tribes and principal-ities not only had considerable autonomy, due to their peripheral location, but, as the empires tried to coerce and coax allegiances in an attempt to ensure frontier security, they had considerable leverage and access to wealth. The imperial conflict was thence to be manifested in shifting tribal loyalties, inter-tribal conflicts and raiding with impunity.[11]

By the 17th century, these manifestations of imperial rivalries had broken Kurdistan into fewer and smaller territories, all constantly scheming against each other. In Persia in the 16th century, Hamadan and Luristan had been detached from Kurdistan, leaving only the Ardelan principality, with its cap-ital at Sanandaj (the principality of Ardelan was abolished in the 1860s, as Iran became increasingly centralized).

The 1746 Treaty of Kurdan followed a further 16 years of full-scale war, during which time the Persians made three attempts to treatise, and con-firmed the 1639 boundary. Nadir Shah of Iran died in the following year, and thus the treaty was not ratified until the 1823 Treaty of Erzerum. In 1806 and 1811 there had been further wars in the area, without a decisive outcome. The imperial powers therefore followed the policy of allowing the area to be semi-independent, therefore functioning as a check to the expan-sion of the rival empire. The status quo was thus more or less maintained, with Kurdistan as almost a third country as a buffer between the feuding parties. This was of course what the empires feared most, a strong and independent Kurdistan. Thus great care was taken to continue the policy of sowing discord in Kurdistan, usually finding the short-sighted principalities fertile ground for their attentions. The Treaty of Erzerum was the first Ottoman–Persian treaty to refer to Kurdistan, and to prohibit imperial med-dling in Kurdish areas across both sides of the border. It is also the first treaty to mention the migration of tribes, and regulations for border cros-sings of people other than pilgrims.[12] The treaty allows for the prevention of raiding and cross-border escapes by certain named tribes,[13] and there is an understanding that cross-border migration, if perceived as a ploy to avoid conscription or evade justice, will be prevented.[14]

The Kurdish principalities had thus far been able to survive by exploiting their buffer location, yet this very location made them vulnerable, and their duplicitous behaviour was to be further exploited by the new powers in the area, initially the Russians, and then the British. During the 19th century, not only was Kurdistan at the margins of the Ottoman and Persian empires, but it was also nudging the Russian empire, thus becoming the theatre for the Russo–Ottoman wars (1804–13, 1828–30, 1877–8). The British became increasingly alarmed by Russian expansionism and favoured the maintenance of Kurdistan as a buffer zone to check the Russians. Thus the British were to collaborate in settling the Ottoman/Persian border dispute to ensure just such a zone and their active involvement in its affairs.[15] The Treaty of Berlin (1878), which concluded the Russo–Ottoman wars, was to provoke Kurdish nationalist feelings, culminating in the attempt to create a united Kurdistan, led by Shaikh Obaydullah, and involving the invasion of Iranian Kurdish territory.[16] This uprising, once it had stifled the Armenian movement, as suited the Ottomans, was suppressed by the combined efforts of the Russians, Iranians, Ottomans and British. The ultimate disadvantage of Kurdistan's location was now obvious. The rival powers have always been able to manipulate the Kurds, and are always able to overcome their differences as a result of their mutual animosity to any real Kurdish gains that may one day result in a loss of territory.

The demarcation of the Turco/Persian boundary

In 1843 Britain and Russia's offer to mediate in the festering Ottoman–Persian territorial dispute was accepted, with the immediate result that a quadripartite boundary delimitation commission was instituted and the ultimate consequence that in 1847 the Treaty of Erzerum was signed, delimiting the boundary along its entire length, albeit in varying degrees of detail and precision. A further commission was set up to establish more precisely the line of boundary on the ground, but the irreconcilable interpretations of the 1847 treaty maintained by the local powers meant that its activity was restricted during 1850–1852 to surveying the tract of land from the Gulf to Ararat in which the boundary lay. In 1869, the wildly inaccurate joint map, the "Carte Identique", was produced, concluding only that an area of 40 kilometres width contained the frontier. Having agreed to "split the difference" over the inaccuracies, the Ottoman and Persian empires eventually accepted that Britain and Russia could arbitrate any remaining dispute over the alignment of the boundary in the 1913 Protocol of Constantinople. It was decided that a Commission of the Four Powers should demarcate the three-quarters of the frontier that was agreed, and decide the last quarter on the ground. This demarcation took 10 months and involved the erection of 227 pillars. Colonel Ryder, the British member of that commission, was well aware that the Kurds were most unreceptive to the demarcation of the boundary:[17] "There's more fun and freedom in the raiding line when no-one knows exactly where the frontier lies. . . The fixing of a frontier was repugnant to the finer feelings of the Kurds."[18] The commission was even attacked by Kurds and shot at, and many of their pillars were uprooted. Sir Arnold Wilson commented that Kurds "have a conception of frontiers which is different from ours but quite reasonable. Sovereignty is not vested in land but in people. Freedom of movement . . . is essential to nomads."[19]

Only two adjustments have been made to the Iranian boundary within Kurdistan. In 1932, the Turks and the Iranians exchanged Iranian territory near to Kotur for Turkish territory west of Urmia and Ararat. In 1937, Iran was given a small favourable adjustment near to Maz Bicho, west of Urmia.

The Kurds of Iran

Ryder highlighted the Kurdish ambivalence to borders. In addition to disliking imposed frontiers, the Kurds depended then, as they do to some extent now, on cross-border raids and smuggling as a way of life.[20] Van Bruinessen considers smuggling to be one of the pillars of the Kurdish economy, ranking its contribution as third, after agriculture and animal husbandry.[21] Yalcin-Heckmann has written extensively about smuggling over the Iran/Turkey border. It has an essential place in the Kurdish lifestyle: economically; as a source of tribal unity; culturally, as a expression of contempt for central power; and politically, as the main source of revenue for illegal political and terrorist groups.[22] Yet, despite this ambivalence, the Kurds in Iran have never really challenged Iran's international borders.

In Iran, the Kurds have always been in a rather different position from that of their Kurdish siblings across the boundaries. The Iranian Kurds were, at least administratively, separated from the rest of Kurdistan for around 300 years before real agitation for a Kurdish state began around the end of the First World War. The Iranian Kurds were never included in any plans for such a state, even by Kurdish leaders within the previous Ottoman territories. There has been only one possibly serious attempt by Iranian Kurds to be united with their fellow Kurds, that of Simko in 1918. This can be viewed however as a primarily tribal power struggle, as Simko was not interested in uniting with those tribes who traditionally opposed his Shakak tribe.[23]

In the past the Kurds have played a substantial rôle in Iran: the country was even ruled by a Kurdish dynasty, the Zands (1752–95). The last independent Kurdish principality in Iran, Ardelan with its capital at Sennah (Sanandaj), ceased to exist after the 1860s. Since that time, the Kurds have been marginalized in the Iranian polity, although probably not more than other ethnic groups on Iran's geographical margins. Despite close family, tribal, religious (via the various Sufi orders) and even economic links across the borders, Iranian Kurds have also been largely willing to view themselves as Iranians, as well as Kurds, as inherently there need be no contradiction in this. Iran is an acknowledged multi-ethnic state, even if minorities are not automatically accorded any special rights. It may be that the Iranian Kurds realize that the international border has never presented an absolute barrier to their activities and contacts, and also have more confidence that the maintenance of Kurdish identity does not necessarily depend on winning statehood.

This acceptance by Iranian Kurds of the concept of a dual identity, that of a participant in the Iranian state and that of an ethnic Kurd, with some degree of cross-border identification, is reflected in the manifestos of all Iranian Kurdish political groupings. The only independent Kurdish territory was established in Iran for one year in 1946. Although the Iranian Kurds were assisted by Barzani's Iraqi Kurds, no attempt was made to extend the Kurdish Republic of Mahabad's territory across international frontiers. The president, Qazi Mohammad, clearly stated that he was an Iranian, and coined the slogan that was to become the main thrust of the Kurdish Democratic Party of Iran: "Autonomy for Kurdistan, *within a democratic Iran*." Even his Pact of Three Borders of August 1944 had allowed only for cross-border contacts and assistance for other Kurds, but not for the subversion of the existing international borders.[24]

Whatever the claims of Iranian Kurds, they have not yet included a reassessment of Iran's external boundaries, only a redrawing of the provincial boundaries to take into account their ethnic makeup. Iran has had a province known as Kurdistan since the 1920s, with Sanandaj as its administrative capital. However, the provinces of west Azerbaijan, Ilam and Kermanshah may well be claimed as having a majority Kurdish population. After the 1979 Iranian revolution, when the Iranian Kurds were waging an all-out war against the central government in the pursuit of autonomy, they even dropped all prior claims to the zone of autonomy, and requested a simple majority popular vote to define the area. No Kurdish political party has failed to declare its attachment to the territorial integrity of Iran. It is clear that the Iranian Kurds have never been radical separatists, and it is also surprising, but true that there has been extremely little cross-border political and military contact between the Kurds in the last 100 years.

There are two main reasons why Iran's 5,500,000 Kurds (10 per cent of the population)[25] may be driven to reassess their moderate demands and to look again at the international frontiers. One is that regional conflict has led to tighter border control, thus largely halting the *de facto* irrelevance of the boundary's whereabouts and also previous cross-border cultural contact. Secondly, the Kurds may begin to feel that moderation pays low dividends, and that they might be more likely to gain their modest aim of autonomy under the control of a more sympathetic government; or more likely when the Iranian government is threatened by a very real possibility of the secession of part of its historic empire.

Notes

1. Captain F. R. Maunsell, "Kurdistan", *The Geographical Journal* (1894), 81–95.
2. Sharaf Al Din Khan of Bitlis, *Sharafnameh*, translated by F. Charmoy (St Petersburg, 1868–76).
3. See M. T. O'Shea, "Greater Kurdistan, the mapping of a myth?" in *Kurdistan – economic and political potential*, M. T. O'Shea (ed.), 1–26 (London: Geopolitical Boundary Research Centre, School of Oriental and African Studies, 1992).
4. D. McDowall, *The Kurds. A nation denied*, 7 (London: Minority Rights Group, 1992).
5. For a detailed description of the ancient history of the Zagros region, see M. R. Izady, *The Kurds: a concise handbook*, 28–34 (London: Taylor & Francis, 1992).
6. Xenophon, *The Persian expedition*, 11–28 (London: Penguin, 1984).
7. Izady, op. cit., 35.
8. Ibid.
9. For example, the Ahl-e-Haq Kurds of Iran practise an apparent form of Zoroastrianism or Yezidism (the only uniquely Kurdish religion), but are labelled Moslems because they have adopted several superficial Islamic features, including veneration of Ali the 4th Caliph.
10. See entry on Kurds in *Encyclopaedia of Islam*, W. C. Brice (ed.), vol. 5, 438–85 (Leiden: E. J. Brill, 1981).
11. T. Y. Ismael, *Iran and Iraq: roots of conflict*, 2 (Syracuse: Syracuse University Press, 1982).
12. Article 1, Treaty of Peace (Erzerum). For full text see J. C. Hurewitz, *Diplomacy in the Near and Middle East*, vol. 1, 90–1 (Princeton: Van Nostrand, 1956).
13. Ibid., Article 3, 91–2.
14. Ibid., Article 4, 92.
15. Ismael, op. cit., 5.
16. R. Olson, *The emergence of Kurdish nationalism and the Sheikh Said rebellion 1880–1925* (Austin: University of Texas Press, 1989).
17. Colonel C. H. D. Ryder, "The demarcation of the Turco/Persian boundary in 1913–14", *Geographical Journal* **65** (1925), 227–37.
18. Ibid., 234.
19. Ibid., 238.
20. Ibid., 227.
21. M. Van Bruinessen, *Agha, sheikh and state*, 190 (London: Zed Books, 1992).
22. L. Yalcin-Heckmann, *Kinship and tribal organisation in the province of Hakkari, southeast Turkey* (PhD thesis, London School of Economics, 1986).
23. M. Van Bruinessen, "Kurdish tribes and the state of Iran: the case of Simko's revolt", in *The conflict of tribe and state in Afghanistan and Iran*, R. Tapper (ed.), 364–96 (London: Croom Helm, 1983).
24. W. Eagleton, *The Kurdish republic of 1946*, 107 (London: Oxford University Press, 1963).
25. McDowall, op. cit., 12.

CHAPTER SIX

Territoriality and the Iran–Iraq war

Keith McLachlan

The geography of the border zone

The long border between the former Persian and Ottoman empires (Fig 6.1) has been much disputed over many centuries.[1] A considerable area of territory changed hands over this protracted period of imperial strife, contained within a vast swathe of land between the Persian Gulf in the south and the Tauris mountains in the north. Subsequent occupations of the borderlands by the two sides inevitably left residual claims across both sides of the contemporary frontier and a legacy of lack of precision on the questions of allegiance of border tribes and the allocation of territory.

The modern border conflict takes its roots at least from the first half of the 16th century as the Ottomans in Asia Minor and the Safavids in Persia sought to establish supremacy. The Persian empire fared badly and after the battle of Calderan in 1514 lost much of its influence in the northwest of the empire.[2] The Accord of Amasya in 1555 confirmed large losses of control of territory by Iran. It laid down that the border was a broad zone rather than a specific line. It was an acknowledgement of the difficulties in defining spheres of influence in a topographically and ethnically complex region and ensured continuing instability of the border area. The Treaty of Constantinople of 1590 formalized this imprecise arrangement, which persisted despite the reannexation of much of Azerbaijan and parts of Kurdistan by Shah Abbas I, ratified by the Treaty of Zohab in 1639. Subsequent negotiations between Ottoman and Persian rulers, including the first Treaty of Erzerum of 1823 and the later interventions of the imperial powers, particularly after 1843 when the joint Ottoman, Persian, Russian and British border delimitation commission was established, failed to remove the ambiguities inherent in the genesis of the broad frontier zone. Other contemporary border problems exhibit similar traits, but this case was complicated by the ambitions of the imperial powers,[3] the discovery of oil[4] and the requirements of economic modernization.

The modern sovereign states of Iran and Iraq have inherited all the ambiguities of the earlier period, apparently with a degree of relish.

Figure 6.1 The Iran/Iraq border, 1993.

The topography of the Iran/Iraq borderlands is extremely varied. In the south it takes the approximate course of the Shatt al-Arab waterway and its adjacent marches across the Mesopotamian plain before striking into the foothills of the Zagros and the high basins such as Mehran. The heights of the Zagros–Tauris ranges increase in altitude and topographic complexity with travel northwards to high mountains in the Tauris proper, where narrow intermontane basins and confined river valleys form the only accesses

58

in difficult terrain. Despite this physical diversity, there is a remarkable singleness of aspect to the border zone – marshland, high hills and mountain have all acted over long periods as negative areas for human settlement.

Malarial marsh in the south, hills difficult to cultivate and isolated from the political centres in the southern Zagros and mountain fastnesses in the north were barriers to occupation by human groups, which reinforced the nature of the area as a periphery between two empires. The only area where this phenomenon was either lacking entirely or less important than elsewhere was Azerbaijan. There lower altitudes and reliable rainfall gave a zone of comparatively dense population for the most part settled, or, if nomads, entirely contained on and with political allegiance to one side of the imperial divide or the other like the Shahsevan of the Dasht-e Moghan.

The geography of human occupance reflects in large measure the effects of topography and history. Small, unco-ordinated and persecuted minorities were pushed into the marsh and mountain redoubts of the borderland, which became havens of refuge. A significant characteristic of society in the border area south of Azerbaijan is nomadism. Kurdish groups of a variety of linguistic and tribal affiliations straddle the border zone in the centre and north, while Arab groups, generally of a semi-nomadic or transhumant type, occupy the southern reaches of the frontier. Scattered and mobile human groups thus existed because of and added to the sense of the region acting as a no-man's-land.

This illusion was reinforced by the pattern of settlement. Other than in Iranian Azerbaijan, the frontier zone lacks major cities and there are remarkably few towns except for the sites of garrisons at Kermanshah and Sulaimaniyah on its strategic periphery or contemporary frontier crossing places such as Qasr-e Shirin.

In the modern period, dating for historical convenience from Riza Shah's centralizing initiatives in Iran from the 1920s[5] and a similar process in Iraq after the revolution against the Hashimite king in 1958,[6] the emergence of nation-states meant a gradual strengthening of the hands of the respective central authorities in the border area. A slow development of roads, security and civil administration changed the nature of the region. The geographical isolation of the no-man's-land gave way gradually to norms dictated from Tehran and Baghdad.

By the same token, the new proximity of central government interests, not through a quasi-buffer zone but directly across the frontier wire, induced a change in the border relationship between Iran and Iraq. The transition was difficult, painful and incomplete by the 1990s.

Iran–Iraq relations, 1958–78

After the revolution in 1958, which brought the Iraqi Hashimite monarchy to an end and ushered in a republic, relations between Iran and Iraq came to be characterized by an overt antagonism that was only occasionally suppressed and, even then, only with difficulty.[7] Innate tensions were compounded by specific and overt political differences. The new socialist republic in Iraq was ideologically diametrically opposed to the 5,000-year-old monarchy in Iran. In foreign affairs, Iran was aligned alongside the United States between 1953 and 1978 while Iraq had developed close links with the Soviet Union after the revolution in 1958. In domestic terms, Iraq created a centrally planned economy in which state organizations controlled the means of production,[8] while Iran pursued a policy of combining state intervention in the economy with private enterprise.[9]

As far as relations between Iran and Iraq were concerned, generalized and ill-defined ideological and cultural tensions were much reinforced by specific disputes over their common borders, such as the control of the Kurdish populations in the border regions and the treatment meted out to their respective expatriate communities. The common border had never been completely demarcated by the original (Anglo–Russian-dominated) Four Party Border Commission in 1914, or by any of its successor commissions. As a result, Iraq claimed small sections of the upper valleys of tributary streams to the Tigris river, which flowed off the Zagros mountains, while Iran had residual claims to areas around Penjwin and elsewhere.

There was also a bitter dispute over the delimitation of the Shatt al-Arab river – the confluence of the Tigris and Euphrates river systems at the head of the Gulf – and over the question of sovereign control over the waterway. This was to prove the touchstone of hostility between the two states. Iran had considered the agreements achieved by international arbitration before the First World War (1913 Constantinople Protocol) and the Second World War (1937 Tehran Treaty) to be profoundly unsatisfactory because they had located the boundary along the low-water mark on the Iranian side of the river except for certain mid-stream regions that acted as anchorages for the Iranian ports of Khorramshahr and Abadan. In 1975, partly as a result of the support provided to Iraqi Kurdish rebels by Tehran, Iran was able to reverse this situation. The Iraqi government, exhausted by its protracted and unsuccessful war in Kurdistan, was forced to concede Iranian claims over the Shatt al-Arab boundary in the Algiers Agreement. Iraqis, however, saw the agreement as a betrayal in which Iran had stolen Iraqi sovereign rights.[10]

The government in Baghdad never abandoned its determination eventually to redress the situation over the control of the Shatt al-Arab. This, however, was only one of several international boundary problems that continued to bedevil relations between Baghdad and Tehran. Another contentious issue that Iraq was exercised to alter was the Iranian occupation of the islands of Abu Musa and the Tunbs since 1971, together with the wider issue of Iran's clear desire to establish its political hegemony over the Gulf region.

It may be argued, therefore, that the matter of borders had been for many years at the heart of Irano–Iraqi rivalries. Other kinds of difficulties arose from time to time to subsume and join with but rarely eclipse the territorial imperative.

The causes of friction, 1978-9

The coming of the Iranian Islamic revolution of 1979 exacerbated political difficulties between Iran and Iraq. It was not immediately evident, however, that this confrontation would necessarily break out into armed conflict. Some commentators, such as Edmund Ghareeb, argued that "talk of an imminent Iranian–Iraqi military confrontation and of continued border clashes is unlikely".[11] He also made the point, however, that, "Iraq's hopes for better relations did not materialise" and that "deep conflicts of national interest existed between the two countries".[12] The vast majority of informed observers nonetheless anticipated that there would be a major conflict sooner or later. The Economist Intelligence Unit (EIU), for example, in reviewing the Gulf war in 1984, took the view that, "During mid-1979 it seemed that the Ba'ath regime had given up its attempt to find a *modus vivendi* with the new Iranian Government under Dr Bazargan."[13]

One important casualty of the renewed tensions was the 1975 Algiers Agreement and the argument that the improved relations between the two countries inaugurated by its signature would survive the revolution quickly lost ground with most commentators. The general view is perhaps best summed up by Richard Schofield:

The Iranian revolution's success in early 1979 in toppling the monarchy was to effect a considerable destabilisation in relations between Tehran and Baghdad. Saddam Hussain's accession as president of Iraq in July of the same year further accelerated such destabilisation. It was by now clear that Iraq's Ba'ath rulers had signed the Algiers Accord as the only viable alternative to their imminent collapse and that, when the power equation was perceived to have altered across the Shatt al-Arab, action would be taken to restore the river to its "rightful owner".[14]

In fact, signs that the situation between Iran and Iraq had begun to deteriorate rapidly were already evident in 1979. Iran seemed prepared for difficult relations with its neighbour and even for military conflict. It has been pointed out that Ayatollah Khomeini had consistently attacked the Ba'ath regime in his speeches from the very beginning of the revolution and had culminated his attacks with threats over the abrogation of the Algiers Accord in September 1979.[15]

The boundary once again became a symbol of Irano–Iraqi hostility, and border incidents occurred with increasing frequency, more than 560 being reported by Iraq in 1979 and 1980.[16] Indeed, the view that "[r]elations with

Iraq began to deteriorate almost immediately after Khomeini's seizure of power"[17] may well be the most unequivocal opinion expressed by contemporary commentators on events in the Gulf at the start of the 1980s, but it accurately encapsulated the sentiments of the majority. In fact, the only relevant issue in 1979 was the estimation of the degree to which relations would worsen and of the likelihood of military confrontations turning into open war. Even commentators such as Ghareeb, while believing that war would not occur, had to admit that the possibility of armed conflict did exist.

The danger of open conflict was underlined at the time by the intensification of military activity along the border, which culminated in repeated air and land border violations. The scale and severity of these violations, particularly given the ideological context, ensured that the crisis in relations between Iran and Iraq was to be quite different from its predecessors. Between February and September 1979, Iraq protested to Iran over 88 violations of its territory or of its diplomatic missions abroad by Iranians. Iran made similar claims. On 2 April 1979, only 50 days after the culmination of the revolution, Iraqi planes violated the air space of the border city of Mehran. The following day, a detachment of the Iraqi army attacked Qasr-e Shirin and on 7 April the oil installations of the city were hit by Iraqi rockets.[18]

The outbreak of war and the boundary issue

In October 1979, the Iraqi government formally threatened to abrogate the Algiers Accord. At the same time, senior Iraqi officials called for the withdrawal of Iranian troops from Abu Musa and the Tunb islands. By the time that war actually broke out, the Iraq government had also formally complained to Iran over more than 560 border incidents during 1979 and 1980. Iran, too, had protested over frequent Iraqi violations of its territory and air space. During 1980, military clashes and air space violations underlined the degree to which relations had deteriorated.

Typical of the assessments that were being made of the situation in the early months of 1980 was the analysis provided by the EIU in February of that year:

Iraq remains most violently antipathetic to Ayatollah Khomeini and his partners. A virulent propaganda war is in progress from Baghdad in support of the Arab guerrillas operating in Khuzestan. It is believed in Tehran that Iraq is actively training and equipping Arab, Kurd and Baluch opposition groups. Iraq has, meanwhile, embarked on a policy of naval expansion designed to make the Iraqi navy the equal of Iran's and is determined to challenge Iran as the major power in the Gulf area in the near future. A number of clashes on the Irano/Iraqi border took place in January, though not between regular troops. Iraqi diplomatic premises in Iran have been occupied and closed, with a number of staff held hostage. Iraq has responded by expelling Iranian nationals on a large scale.[19]

It appeared that there were growing fears in Iraq that the Iranian regime would use Shi'a revolutionary groups inside Iraq to undermine the Ba'ath government. In addition, Baghdad had concluded that the time had also come to recover the territory and prestige that had been lost as a result of the 1975 Algiers Accord and took little care to conceal its views. A rapid and visible rearmament programme began and in January 1980 the government of Iraq signed an agreement with French aircraft manufacturers to increase the supply of Mirage jet fighters.

During March and April 1980, there were growing tensions between the two sides and the dangers of confrontation were significantly increased. In April, Ayatollah Khomeini called upon the Iraqi armed forces to "leave your barracks . . . get rid of Saddam Hussein like we got rid of the shah". Iraq, for its part, intensified its demands for the withdrawal of Iranian forces from Abu Musa and the Tunbs. It also attended to domestic security in characteristically brutal fashion, with the arrest on 5 April and execution some months later of the spiritual leader of the Iraqi Shi'a community and Ayatollah Khomeini's personal representative, Imam Muhammad Baqr Sadr. After the senior Ba'ath official, Tariq Aziz, who was also foreign minister, was the target of an unsuccessful assassination attempt in April, Iraq began the mass deportation of Iraqis of Iranian origin.

There seemed to be little doubt that the Iranian and Iraqi governments were mutually seeking to embarrass and overthrow the other. The situation worsened during the summer, with Iraq apparently increasingly determined that, "by inflicting a severe military defeat on Iran, [it] could undo the Algiers agreement, discredit the revolutionary regime and, perhaps, even establish a client government in Tehran".[20] In July and August 1980, the international media were reporting high levels of Iranian- and Iraqi-sponsored guerrilla activities on both sides of the border. Armed conflict between the regular armed forces of both sides also increased during the same period, particularly in Kurdistan.

The course of the 1980–88 war and the land boundary

The Iran–Iraq conflict acquired two interrelated but separate geographical aspects – first, the land and air war that began in 1980 in the joint boundary zone and, secondly, the crisis in the Persian Gulf itself, which began in 1984 when Iraq declared an exclusion zone and began to attack Gulf shipping in an attempt to cripple the Iranian economy. The events of 1987 in the Gulf, with the US intervention, ostensibly to protect the right of freedom of navigation, and concomitant actions by other Western powers and the USSR, internationalized this conflict to such an extent that it had a virtually independent existence from the land war. The participants differed and the objectives of those involved had little to do with those of the primary protagonists – victory for Iran, avoidance of defeat for Iraq. Indeed, this divergence was so significant that an end to each of the conflicts depended on factors that were quite different in each case. The implications for Iran's international frontiers, however, arose almost entirely from the land war and this review will be concerned mainly with this arena rather than with the later larger-scale crisis.

The course of the war

Hostilities began in September 1980. The war between Iran and Iraq passed through definable phases in which the military initiative changed hands. Although the Iranian military response to the Iraqi invasion was slow to halt the actual penetration of Iranian territory at first, there was an increasing tempo of Iranian initiative and success after 1982.[21] For Tehran, the war became one of *jihad*, while for Baghdad political and national survival became the dominant theme. Yet, Iran's ability to strike a decisive blow was called increasingly into question, both in terms of Iraq's remarkable ability to mobilize international aid to support its military defence and in terms of the success of the Iraqi airforce in interdicting Iranian oil exports after August 1985. It was here that the interrelation between the land and air war and the maritime crisis in the Gulf became most acute and it was also here that the dangers of internationalization of the conflict were in their most threatening form.

The intensifying dispute between Iran and Iraq erupted into full-scale warfare in September 1980, signalled by the Iraqi invasion of Iran. A rapid initial drive into Iranian territory ensured that the Iraqi army occupied the area in Kurdistan around the town of Qasr-e Shirin. In the south there were invasions of Khuzistan with thrusts towards Andimeshk, the central lowlands and, above all, the Iranian port city of Khorramshahr.[22] Hand-to-hand fighting eventually left Khorramshahr considerably damaged but in the possession of the Iraqis. An attempt to take Abadan was eventually frustrated but only after the town was badly mauled and the famous Abadan refinery severely damaged. The Iraqis bombed other Iranian oil facilities and artillery fire rendered much of the steel and other associated industry useless. Large numbers of Iranians were made homeless. It is estimated that more than 1 million Iranians were driven out of the war zone to seek shelter in Tehran and other inland cities.

In combination with Iraqi caution, confused war aims and military incompetence, the Iranian side did enough, nonetheless, to slow down and eventually stop the Iraqi advance.[23] Iraqi units allowed themselves to become tied down in urban fighting in Khorramshahr and Abadan in a style of warfare at which the Iranian irregulars of the revolutionary guards were past masters and which dissipated Iraqi advantages of mobility and fire power. Furthermore, although Iran suffered from the loss of Abadan and Khorram-shahr (which was the country's main port), other likely targets in the oil industry survived untouched by the Iraqi advance. The bulk of oil produc-tion continued unimpaired at this stage and oil export facilities at Kharg island were unaffected by the fighting.

The lack of clarity in Iraqi war aims became clear during 1981. Iraqi forces dug in around Khorramshahr and elsewhere in a narrow strip of territory seized from Iran. It seemed to be assumed in Baghdad that this would be enough to force the Iranians to the conference table and to concede both navigation rights on the Shatt al-Arab and the ownership of the islands of Abu Musa and the two Tunbs. A short period of apparent stalemate occur-red in 1981 but in the second half of the year the Iranian armed forces de-veloped new tactics based on mass infantry assaults against specific sections of Iraqi defences, regardless of losses in men and equipment.[24] The Iraqis held to static defensive positions and were quite unable to cope with this new Iranian tactic. Iraqi lines began gradually to crumble. Growing numbers of Iraqi soldiers gave up without a fight.

The momentum of Iranian attacks grew rapidly and Iraqi frontline units were inched back from Abadan and other forward positions in the south in preparation for a final stand at Khorramshahr. In the event, the battle at Khorramshahr was short lived, for Iraqi commanders wisely opted out of a threatened street-by-street struggle and, with the withdrawal of the defeated units there, the main Iraqi invasion attempt came to an end.

At this point, the Iraqi leadership attempted to negotiate with their Iranian counterparts for a termination of the fighting on terms that, although appreci-ably short of unconditional surrender, gave Iran all that it had previously claimed on the Shatt al-Arab and which dropped references to the Iranian occupation of the islands in the Gulf. It was promised that Iraqi troops would be unilaterally withdrawn from much of the southern front in May 1982 as a gesture designed to encourage a peaceful solution of the conflict.

The war of Islamic jihad

The Iranian leadership was unmoved by Iraqi offers of peace, however. There was a fear that Iraq would merely use a ceasefire and peace negoti-ations as a means of preparing for a new attack on Iran. In any case, the Iraqi withdrawal was seen in Tehran as incomplete. Iraqi troops remained on Iranian territory in the northern sector near to Mehran and Qasr-e Shirin and at other locations. There were also undoubtedly Islamic groups in Tehran that foresaw that a military victory in Iraq would open up the heart-land of the Islamic world to reform carried by the Iranian sword. The ideals of Ayatollah Khomeini and the Islamic revolution, it was believed, could be translated into reality over a wide geographical area at little cost.

On 13 July 1982 the Iranians began a major land attack against Iraqi defences around Basra. The Iranians were surprised, however, by the resistance put up by their enemies. The Iraqi ranks did not break and very heavy casualties were inflicted on the attacking Iranian forces. The Iraqis remained firm in the defence of their territory and the war settled into one of attrition.

The pattern of Iranian massed attacks against the Iraqi frontline continued into 1983, with a major offensive launched in February against Al-Amarah. In July the frustrations of the war in the lowlands of the south were compensated by a new front opened in Kurdistan. The Iranians pushed into Iraqi territory around the highlands of Hajj Omran, taking a number of critical peaks in the region. A similar attack on Penjwin, a valley salient in the northern front, was also carried out with some limited success.

The Iranian offensive started in 1984 with a diversionary attack on the Darbandi Khan area of Kurdistan in February, when the Iraqis were caught by surprise and pushed back from a number of commanding heights. Immediately in the wake of this skirmishing in the north the Iranians launched a large-scale offensive in the south against Al-Qurnah, using massed infantry in light and amphibious transport to spearhead a breakthrough aimed at crossing the Tigris. It seemed initially that the Iranians might succeed when some small detachments did reach the banks of the Tigris. However, an Iraqi counter-attack, using armour and air support, left the Iranians in control of only small areas of the marshlands around Majnun oilfield. In short, Iranian claims that they would make a final strike against Iraq were not fulfilled.

Iran's opportunity for military victory appeared to be slipping away by 1984. The danger was recognized in Tehran but was not accepted as sufficient grounds for seeking a peaceful solution. The much-improved Iraqi performance behind defence entrenchments along the front was countered by the mobilization of even larger numbers of Iranian frontline troops, with some three-quarters of a million men under arms in the southern front region alone. This vast assembly was ultimately deployed on 11 March 1985 in the Hawizah marshlands when amphibious columns broke through Iraqi lines and pushed forward to the west bank of the Tigris. The Iraqi forces appeared to be in difficulties for a short time but recovered rapidly and eventually drove back Iranian troops with heavy losses. In 1986, the seventh year of the war, Iran continued to show both stubbornness and imagination in its prosecution of the conflict. On 10 February, Iranian armed forces successfully crossed the Shatt al-Arab and seized the small and lightly defended Iraqi outport of Fao. While the port itself was of little value and had not functioned since the beginning of the war, the crossing changed the geography of the land war, giving Iran a foothold on the peninsula south of Basra city and a military position just across the waters of the Khor Abdulla inlet from Kuwaiti territory. Iran obtained other incidental benefits from the Fao landing, including the costs suffered by the Iraqi army from its completely inept and expensive attempts to relieve the town and the enormous psychological affront the landings gave to the Arab states of the Gulf. Kuwait in particular was brought directly into the area of conflict.[25]

The Iraqis attempted to salvage their pride with a strike against Iranian positions at Mehran but failed to hold the city itself in the face of an Iranian counter-attack. Further small-scale skirmishing continued in the north around Hajj Omran during the year but without altering the real position in the area. The Iranian leadership called for the year 1365 (ending 20 March 1987) to be one of "destiny" in which the war would be successfully brought to an end. Very large numbers of Iranian troops were assembled in the south to threaten the Iraqis with a new major offensive. On 23 December, the Karbala 4 offensive began with a crossing of Iranian troops to the island of Umm al-Rassas opposite Khorramshahr. The attack was repulsed, but the Iraqi forces did not realize that the attack was to be only a prelude to a full-scale offensive, which occurred shortly afterwards.[26]

The great assault on Basra in 1987

A large Iranian army, gathered in the south during the second half of 1986, was eventually brought into play on 10 January 1987 when the Karbala 5 offensive was launched. Revolutionary guard battalions fought their way through Iraqi defences to the east of Basra, using the former border post at Shalamcheh as their starting point and moving onto ground commanding Basra adjacent to the artificial Fish Lake created by the Iraqis as water defences for the north and northeast of the city. The Iraqi outer defences did not hold out against the attacks, and it appeared at one stage in mid-January that the Iranians might be able to break through into the outskirts of Basra itself. Iraqi use of air power was expensive since the Iranians were in possession of advanced US and other anti-aircraft missiles.

Ultimately, however, the Iranians were unable to sustain their drive towards Basra. Iraqi forces pushed them back into the marshes, leaving the Iranians with only an estimated 150 km^2 to show for their approximately 45,000 dead. Later attempts by the Iranian armed forces in April to regain ground lost to the Iraqis were generally unsuccessful. In parallel with the Karbala 5 operations there was also an Iranian attack in the north on the Sumar area in association with Iraqi Kurdish guerrillas. The Iranian armed forces eventually gave up their thrust towards Basra. Other than a brief attack by revolutionary guards in April to try to push back the advance of the Iraqis in the Fish Lake area, the Iranians were unable to follow through their early gains. Iraq once again recovered.

It will be clear from this discussion of the events of the land war that the territorial ambit of the Iran–Iraq war was extremely limited. Other than for short periods of aerial bombardment affecting inland towns and cities, the geography of the war was confined to a very narrow strip of land adjacent to the shared boundary. Iraq never seriously attempted to penetrate the

Iranian central plateau. Iran's efforts at driving its forces through to the Tigris–Euphrates or even Basra were unsuccessful. In many ways the war was akin to a border conflict and, despite the contention that friction over the border was no more than an expression of deeper national conflicts,[27] it was remarkable that not only was the land war contained within the border perimeter but, as will be shown later, post-war negotiations ultimately pivoted around the question of land and the ownership of the Shatt al-Arab waterway rather than any other single issue.

The US intervention and the internationalization of the crisis

The Gulf crisis proper can be tied to the decision by the United States to take a unilateral initiative in the Gulf. The formula used by the USA was to take responsibility for the safety of Kuwaiti tanker traffic in the Gulf by the re-flagging of Kuwaiti vessels under the American flag. This had the added advantage of pre-empting the Kuwaiti move towards using Soviet protection for the same purpose. Some 11 Kuwaiti tankers were to be re-flagged and, on 16 July 1987, the re-flagging procedures were completed on the crude carrier *Bridgetown*, formerly the *Al-Rekkah*, and the gas carrier *Gas Prince*, formerly the *Minagish*. In July, the Kuwaitis also began the process of re-flagging and chartering other vessels under the British flag.

The re-flagging of tankers and other craft in July was, in part at least, due to the culmination of anger and frustration in the international community on the matter of the Gulf war. The Iranians appear to have made a bad mistake in misreading the mood of the USA in particular and the West in general on the issue.

The internationalization of the Gulf issue was finally formalized on 20 July 1987 when the United Nations Security Council unanimously adopted resolution 598 calling on the belligerents in the Gulf war to end all hostilities. The resolution gave considerable assistance to the USA in convincing its allies that their action in policing the Gulf was legal and in engaging support from the world community at large. It succeeded, too, in isolating Iran[28] so that, however much Tehran might be evasive in the matter, it would be clearly confronted with an international demand to state publicly whether it accepted an end to the war or not.

The Iranian response to UN resolution 598 was to prevaricate. Tehran attempted to make its offers of peace conditional on a shifting set of demands, which appeared to vary, depending on which particular leader was articulating them. A reply by the Iranians to Señor Perez de Cuellar, the UN Secretary General, on 11 August 1987, was vague and seen as a further attempt at diverting the UN from its declared purpose of achieving a ceasefire.

In effect, during early 1987 the Iranians allowed the air war in the Persian Gulf to become a weapon against their interests. The leadership in Tehran rather unwittingly opened the way for external intervention. Within a few months the Gulf was turned from an Iranian controlled area into one where the Iranians were surrounded on all sides. The loss of military dominance in the Gulf marked a change in the Iranian potential for pursuing the war against Iraq.

The Iranian position deteriorated rapidly during 1988. In the land war the country had run out of options. Shortages beset the regime on all sides. By 1988 it was clear to all but a few in Tehran that the fighting ability of the armed forces was poor. This was finally publicly recognized by the Iranian political establishment in July 1988, when a much-belated acknowledgement was given that the army command needed making more coherent, that events were moving indisputably against the Islamic republic and that peace was urgently needed. On 20 July, the president formally wrote to accept UN resolution 598.

The speed of the ultimate Iranian military collapse was unexpected. The damage of more than seven years of warfare had dissipated all the advantages that Iran had originally possessed. It was also true that failures in the field of foreign affairs and economy had exacerbated difficulties in the military arena.

For the Iranians, the Gulf crisis had made enemies without bringing any notable gains. For the peace lobby in Iran, the US intervention indicated that the Iranians would never be allowed to win the war either in the Gulf or elsewhere. In this there was an ironic utility, since this argument for ending the war enabled Ayatollah Khomeini to accept the UN ceasefire when perhaps other forms of pressure would have failed to move him.

The post-war border settlement

In accepting UN resolution 598 on 18 July 1988 the Iranian authorities looked for settlement under UN auspices of four key issues: imposition of a formal peace, which would include the return of all prisoners of war; relapse of all international border questions to the *status quo ante*; determination of responsibility for the start of the war; and payment of war reparations.

During the period from August 1988 to August 1990 Iran was in a relatively weak position vis-à-vis Iraq on all these issues because of its palpable military and economic weaknesses. Iran accepted a ceasefire on 8 August, which became effective on 20 August, 1988. Implementation of UN resolution 598 was slow, however. Iraq demanded that Iran join in face-to-face negotiations, at that stage an anathema to the Islamic republic. Talks in Geneva in November 1988 made no progress, largely, it seemed, because Iraq demanded the rescinding of the 1975 Algiers Accord and a return of control of navigation on the Shatt al-Arab to the terms laid down in the 1937 agreement. Deadlock between the two sides persisted, since Iran required the withdrawal of all Iraqi troops from the 2,600 km^2 of Iranian territory it claimed was still occupied before beginning general negotiations, while Iraq refused to move until normal navigation was restored on the Shatt al-Arab. In practice, the only formal advances made after the ceasefire were the posting of forces of the United Nations Iran-Iraq Military Observation Group (UNIIMOG) to supervise the military front and the exchange of small numbers of prisoners of war.

In January 1990 Iraq made a three-point peace proposal to Iran including direct talks, an immediate exchange of prisoners of war and the reopening of the joint border to all nationals, but, implicitly, with the Algiers Accord open for renegotiation. Iran rejected this initiative but suggested an alternative, seven-point plan, which demanded an immediate and simultaneous withdrawal of troops behind pre-existing international borders and the full implementation of UN resolution 598. Indeed, the border issue remained as the main area of disagreement, being the key Iranian objection to a new Iraqi peace proposal on 1 May. Iranian and Iraqi foreign ministers met in Geneva for direct talks on 4 July 1990, though little progress was made.

On 2 August 1990 Iraq invaded Kuwait. This prompted the opening of a new phase in the Iran-Iraq dispute. Iraqi officials travelled to Tehran in the aftermath of the invasion, and on 15 August it was announced in Baghdad that Iranian conditions for a peace to end the Iran-Iraq war would be accepted in full, once the situation with respect to the Iraqi annexation of Kuwait was confirmed. In fact, Iraqi spokesmen indicated that all their troops would be withdrawn from territory claimed by Iran, that prisoners of war would be returned and that the Algiers Accord on the Shatt al-Arab would be reconfirmed. Only payment of war reparations and attribution of responsibility for the start of the war in September 1980 were omitted from the Iraqi list, indicating that, even in the pressured circumstances of the post-invasion period, Iraq did not entirely and publicly accept resolution 598.

Unfortunately, the offers made by Baghdad at that period were never ratified. Some permanent gains were made by Iran by way of freedom of movement of pilgrims to the Shi'a shrines, the reopening of communications links and re-establishment of diplomatic relations. In January 1991 the two sides moved their armed forces back 1km from the frontline under a UN-arranged withdrawal, and the UNIIMOG teams ceased to function from February of the same year. Thus some of the tensions along the front were diffused.

But the promises made by Iraq in August 1990 lapsed in the wake of the collapse of Iraq before the Allied forces in the Arabian peninsula in January–February 1991. The outstanding issues of the alignment of the international frontier, control of land adjacent to the border and the status of the Shatt al-Arab remained unsettled. UN resolution 598 was not implemented other than to effect a ceasefire and partial separation of forces. The Iran-Iraq border question thus persisted both as a potential *casus belli* of a general kind as envisaged by Ancel[29] but more threateningly as an existing cause of friction in its own right.

Notes

1. K. S. McLachlan, "Iranian boundaries with the Ottoman Empire", in *Encyclopaedia Iranica*, E. Yar Shater (ed.), vol. 4, 401–3 (New York: Routledge, 1989); R. N. Schofield, "Iran's borders with Turkey", in *Encyclopaedia Iranica*, 415–17 (1989).
2. R. K. Ramazani, *The foreign policy of Iran: a developing nation in world affairs, 1500–1941* (Charlottesville: University Press of Virginia, 1966).
3. M. Yapp, "1900–21: the last years of the Qajar dynasty", in *Twentieth century Iran*, E. Amirsadeghi (ed.), 11–2 (London: Heinemann, 1977).
4. R. Ferrier, *Note on the transferred territories* (undated, London: British Petroleum).
5. W. Knapp, "1921–41: the period of Riza Shah", in Amirsadeghi, op. cit., 35.
6. P. Marr, *The modern history of Iraq*, 179–80 (Boulder: Westview, 1985).
7. Ibid.
8. M. Khadduri, *Republican Iraq* (London: Royal Institute of International Affairs, 1969).
9. J. Bharier, *Economic development in Iran, 1900–1970*, 101 (Oxford: Oxford University Press, 1971).
10. T. Y. Ismael, *Iraq and Iran: roots of conflict* (Syracuse: Syracuse University Press).
11. E. Ghareeb, "Iraq: emergent oil power", in *The security of the Persian Gulf*, H. Amirsadeghi (ed.), 216 (London: Croom Helm, 1981).
12. Ibid.
13. K. S. McLachlan & E. G. H. Joffé, *The Gulf war*, 32 (London: Economic Intelligence Unit, 1984).
14. R. N. Schofield, *Evolution of the Shatt al-Arab boundary dispute*, 64 (London: Menas Press, 1986).
15. A. H. Cordesman, *The Gulf and the search for regional strategic stability*, 661–5 (Boulder: Westview/Mansell, 1984).
16. A. Drysdale & G. Blake, *The Middle East and North Africa: a political geography* (Oxford: Oxford University Press, 1985).
17. S. Zabih, *Iran since the revolution*, 176 (London: Croom Helm, 1982).
18. Islamic Republic of Iran, *The imposed war* (Tehran: Islamic Republic of Iran, 1984).
19. Economic Intelligence Unit, *Iran; quarterly economic review*, 10–1 (London: EIU, 1980).
20. S. Bakhash, *The reign of the Ayatollahs*, 127 (London: I. B. Tauris, 1985).
21. McLachlan & Joffé, op. cit., 42–4.
22. Cordesman, op. cit., 661–5.
23. M. S. El-Azhary, "Introduction", in *The Iran–Iraq war*, M. S. El-Azhary (ed.), 2–3 (London: Croom Helm, 1984).
24. B. R. Kuniholm, *Persian Gulf and United States policy*, 76–7 (Claremont: Regina, 1984).
25. W. E. White, "The Iran–Iraq war: a challenge to the Arab Gulf states", in *Crosscurrents in the Gulf*, H. R. Sindelar III & J. E. Peterson (eds), 97 (London: Routledge, 1988).
26. Economic Intelligence Unit, *Iran country report* 1 & 2 (London: EIU, 1987).
27. J. Ancel, *Les frontières* (Paris: Galliard, 1936).
28. *Annual register*, Iran, 288 (London: Longman, 1988).
29. Ancel, op. cit.

CHAPTER SEVEN

Interpreting a vague river boundary delimitation
The 1847 Erzerum treaty and the Shatt al-Arab before 1913

RICHARD SCHOFIELD

Introduction

When arriving or trying to arrive at a final agreement with neighbouring states over the status and alignment of international borders, many modern Middle Eastern states have been troubled by the unsatisfactory definition of original delimitations. These were drawn up typically at a much earlier stage by European colonial powers, or, as is the case in this chapter dealing with the Persian Qajar and Ottoman empires, by European imperial powers with a strong degree of leverage over the area. This is true of both inter-state land borders running overland and those running along rivers. The line of the Kuwait/Iraq boundary demarcated by a United Nations team as recently as November 1992 was essentially an interpretation of the vague and ambiguous wording of an Anglo–Ottoman territorial understanding that has survived to constitute the legal definition of this limit since 1913.[1] Divided international rivers are rare in the Middle Eastern region, but the same problems of reconciling poor textual definitions to the physical features they supposedly describe have been experienced in all instances. If, as a result of the current "peace process", Israel ultimately arrives at final border settlements with its Arab neighbours, use will undoubtedly be made of the original definitions that introduced the territorial limits of mandated Palestine. With Jordan, eventual agreement on the boundary along the River Jordan will be based upon a vague stipulation of 1922 that the delimitation should run along the "centre" of that river.[2] Fortunately, even by 1922, certain important ground rules had been established concerning where boundaries should run along international rivers. The Versailles treaties of 1919 prescribed that international boundaries running along navigable rivers should assume a *thalweg* delimitation, that is along the line of continuous deepest soundings.[3] At the same time, a median line delimitation was deemed more suitable for non-navigable international rivers.

72

In the period before the Great War only one territorial limit in the region had seriously preoccupied the imperial powers – the long-established Perso–Ottoman marches from the Persian Gulf to the Transcaucasus.[4] Britain and Russia's strategic need for territorial stability in these borderlands had led to their direct intervention in the Perso–Ottoman dispute by the early 1840s. Their mediation efforts ultimately resulted in the conclusion of the second Treaty of Erzerum (1847) and the Constantinople Protocol (1913), which together defined a boundary along the entire length of the border march from Mount Ararat in the north to the mouth of the Shatt al-Arab in the south. After London and St Petersburg had been vested with powers to arbitrate in any future dispute over the precise alignment of the boundary, this delimitation was demarcated in 1914.

Problematic 20th-century experiences of equating inadequate border definitions with the features they describe are as nothing compared with the tribulations of those charged between 1850 and 1913 with plotting more precisely the boundary delimitation introduced for the Shatt al-Arab by the Erzerum treaty of 1847. While this instrument with its explanatory notes is usually regarded as having introduced a boundary for the Shatt al-Arab along its eastern (Persian) shore (certainly this seemed to be Britain's view at the time), control of the river itself was not even mentioned in the 1847 treaty, merely control of land to its immediate east. Britain's general insistence in the period up until 1913 that a river boundary delimitation had been introduced by a treaty which had made no mention of that river's sovereignty certainly set the stage for considerable dispute and confusion, not least amongst its own government officials. Perhaps it was little wonder that Mr G. E. Hubbard, Secretary to the British delegation on the Turco–Persian Frontier Commission of 1914, later described the Perso–Ottoman territorial dispute as "a phenomenon of procrastination unparalleled in the chronicles of oriental diplomacy".[5]

The efforts of British officials of the India and Home governments to establish more clearly the line introduced at Erzerum and to equate this, during the early 20th century, with the most practical line in regional terms, are the subject of this chapter. It is divided into two parts: the first examines the negotiation, conclusion and subsequent difficulties caused by the 31 May 1847 Treaty of Erzerum; the second focuses upon the development of the Shatt al-Arab question in the years preceding the 1913 Constantinople Protocol, a period in which the India Office and the Foreign Office were at loggerheads over the question of what constituted the proper boundary delimitation along the river. Three particular interpretations and observations are crucial: the Williams line of 1850 (see Fig. 7.2); the locally recognized frontier observed by Wilson in 1909 (see Fig. 7.3); and Grey's compromise boundary solution of 1912 (see Fig. 7.4).

On the face of it, there would, in the autumn of 1993, seem to be little practical value in reviewing the territorial arrangement introduced for the Shatt al-Arab by the 1847 Treaty of Erzerum. Two weeks into its invasion of Kuwait in mid-August 1990 and having claimed the Shatt al-Arab as an Iraqi "national river" ever since its manoeuvrings prior to launching the 1980–8 Iran–Iraq war, Iraq suddenly signalled its readiness to accept once again a *thalweg* delimitation along the Shatt al-Arab river, as had originally been introduced by the 1975 Algiers Accord package of agreements signed between Iran and Iraq. Iran wasted no opportunity in publicizing Iraq's strategically motivated climbdown but must be aware even so, since no formal document has been signed to follow up this development, that it was factors extraneous to the Shatt dispute itself that were responsible for Iraqi President Saddam Hussain's turnaround. This was, of course, also the case back in 1975, when the Shah's promises to cease support for the Kurdish rebellion in northern Iraq had ultimately caused Hussain (then vice-president) to agree to Iran's long-standing positional demand – prosecuted consistently since the late 1920s – that the Shatt al-Arab be delimited by the *thalweg*. Until Iraq formally revokes its unilateral abrogation (made during September 1980) of the Algiers Accord and puts pen to a new joint document officially recording its unequivocal acceptance of the *thalweg* delimitation introduced by the 1975 treaty, the Shatt dispute must be considered as dormant rather than permanently settled.[6]

It might also be stated at the outset that there is an old Iranian argument, put forward most notably early during 1935 at the Perso–Iraqi debate before the League of Nations in Geneva, whereby the reference to "free navigation rights" for Persian vessels in Article 2 of the 1847 Erzerum treaty had the effect of dividing the river on an equal basis between the Ottoman and Persian empires. Specifically, the clause relating to navigation "without let or hindrance" has been interpreted as indicating that both riparians had an equal right of sovereignty as far as the middle of the river.[7] The same argument was rendered faithfully to this author by Iranian Foreign Ministry officials in Tehran as recently as November 1989. Certainly, at the time of the Erzerum treaty's conclusion, Britain was of the opinion that the Shatt al-Arab was an Ottoman river. By the end of the first decade of the 20th century, as we shall discover, Secretary of State Sir Edward Grey, fully aware by this stage that a mid-stream Shatt boundary was recognized by locals at the head of the Gulf, was not so sure. Traditionally the counter to the Iranian "without let and hindrance" argument has been as follows: had sovereignty been divided or shared, there would have been no need to single out Persian vessels in a stipulation relating to free passage.

The 19th-century evolution of the Shatt al-Arab boundary

Early Perso–Ottoman truces and the indeterminate border march, 1639–1823
Perhaps no single boundary possesses a longer history than that separating Iran and Iraq. This boundary has long displayed the classic characteristics

of a *political frontier*[8] zone or a *border march*. It has been defined and re-defined for over 350 years. The 1639 "Treaty of peace and demarcation of frontiers (Zohab)" remains, certainly in name, the earliest explicitly territor-ial agreement signed between Middle Eastern states. Yet this and subse-quent treaties signed at Hamadan (1727), Kurdan (1746) and Erzerum (1823) were essentially little more than momentary truces in a long religious war between the Sunni Ottoman empire and successive Shi'i Persian dynas-ties.[9] As far as the allocation of territory was concerned, all these instru-ments could do was to identify a wide strip of land in which the authority of both Sultan and Shah was weak and disputed.[10] They made no attempt to allocate territory in the deltaic lands at the head of the Persian Gulf.[11]

Instability and imperial intervention, 1837–43

During the 18th century, effective control of the Shatt al-Arab and its banks as far north as Basra lay with the Ka'b Arabs. This practically autonomous principality was at its most powerful and possessed its greatest territorial ex-tent (from Bubiyan island in the southwest to Ahwaz in the northeast) un-der the energetic leadership of Shaikh Salman Sultan (1737–67). The famous Danish traveller Carsten Niebuhr visited the head of the Persian Gulf in the mid-1760s, commenting that the Ka'b chief had "made himself master of all the isles between the mouths of the Euphrates, commonly called the country of the Schat el Arab".[12]

Under Salman the Ka'b maintained virtual independence in the delta region by playing off the Ottomans and Persians against one another.[13] East India Company records speak of a flourishing Ka'b economy centred upon irrigated agriculture and trade, with taxes levied on shipping using the Shatt al-Arab and Gulf waters to its immediate south. It was perhaps the latter development that persuaded the distant Persian and Ottoman centres of government, as well as the East India Company, that the precocious Salman was a threat to commercial and strategic interests that could no longer be tolerated. After the Ka'b had sprung a surprise by defeating the Ottoman Basra fleet in the mid-1760s, Constantinople sided first with the East India Company and then with the Qajars themselves in an attempt to destroy the dynasty. Though none of these alliances proved conclusive, the result was that all of the Ka'b's energies were expended in survival and a diminished Ka'b territory was preserved only by the abandonment of previ-ously vital economic assets. Nowhere was this symbolized more clearly than with the cutting of the dykes that had irrigated the lowland plains in the delta region, up until the mid-1760s the mainstay of the Ka'b economy.[14] From this point onwards the Ka'b, centred at Muhammara (Khorramshahr), lost some of their effective autonomy with a developing link with central authority in Persia increasingly discernible.

Between 1837 and 1842, the Ottoman Pasha of Baghdad, Ali Riza, twice levelled the Ka'b-controlled port of Muhammara, which was claimed by both the Ottoman Porte and the Qajars. The Ottoman authorities were clearly concerned at this stage that a commercial port outside of their direct administration – whether controlled by the Ka'b or the Persians – could threaten the omnipotence of Basra in the region.[15] A Perso–Ottoman war was averted only with the intervention of Britain and Russia. Britain may well have considered that further serious clashes – there had been serious incidents in the northern border zone as well as Muhammara – would weaken the two combatants in dangerously close proximity to its expansionist rival. Russia itself was keen to maintain tranquillity in its newly acquired provinces of Armenia and Georgia. Britain was also doubtless aware of the threat posed by further warfare to its fast-developing commercial interests in Mesopotamia. It was particularly keen to develop a shorter imperial route to India. Specifically coveted was a mixed communications link running overland from the eastern Mediterranean to Baghdad and then by steamship to the Persian Gulf along the Tigris and Shatt al-Arab.[16]

So, in the spring of 1843 Britain and Russia offered their mediation of the Muhammara question and other existing territorial disputes between the Ottoman empire and Persia. Both sides accepted their offer and the Turco–Persian Boundary Commission was formed, comprising delegates from both the local and the European powers.

Major Rawlinson's memorandum of January 1844

As a direct result, 18 sessions of the quadripartite boundary commission were held between May 1843 and March 1844 at Erzerum, an Ottoman Armenian town in eastern Anatolia. Where the subject of international limits to territory at the head of the Persian Gulf was dwelt upon, discussion centred on the disputed ownership of the port of Muhammara rather than the sovereignty of the Shatt al-Arab itself, which was presumed somewhat unquestioningly by the British and Russian governments to belong to the Ottoman Porte.[17] Informal control of the alluvial flats south and east of Muhammara had, as we have seen, been generally, if intermittently, the preserve of the Ka'b tribe for well over a century.[18] Both the Ottomans and the Persians claimed the allegiance of the Arab Ka'b tribe to support their respective claims to Muhammara at the conferences held at Erzerum. In late 1843, Colonel Williams, the British representative at the conferences, considered that on the strength of evidence at his disposal the Porte had a very strong claim to Muhammara.[19] However, the findings of Major Rawlinson, British Consul at Baghdad, in his memorandum of January 1844 led to a British proposal that Persian sovereignty over Muhammara be recognized by the Porte.

Rawlinson disclosed that the dependency of the Ka'b tribe on the Porte had in effect ceased with their defeat of the Ottoman fleet in 1765 and that during the first half of the 19th century a direct political link had been established between a Ka'b-controlled Muhammara and Persia.[20] On the basis of his findings Rawlinson recommended a frontier delimitation for the delta region (Fig. 7.1). Running northwards, this passed lengthways through the centre of Khizr (Abadan) island, then skirted the town of Muhammara, leaving it to Persia, and then assumed a delimitation running parallel to the Shatt al-Arab at some distance east of the river bank. In recommending this line to Britain's mediating partner, Russia, in the summer of 1844, Sir Stratford Canning, the British ambassador in Constantinople, concluded that the Porte's original right to Muhammara had been superseded by Persia's more recently established right of conquest and possession.[21] Canning also noted that, as far as the Shatt al-Arab was concerned, the Persians could not navigate any part of its course without the levy of shipping duties by the Ottoman authorities.

Count Nesselrode's proposal of September 1844

The Russian vice-chancellor, Count Nesselrode, responded in September 1844 by arguing that Persian sovereignty should be extended not just over Muhammara but right up to the left (eastern) bank of the Shatt al-Arab.[22] As it was already apparent that the Bahmanshir Channel was silting up rapidly, Nesselrode also suggested that Persia be accorded rights of free navigation on the Shatt al-Arab, which, it was judged, would soon become the River Karun's sole outlet to the Persian Gulf.

Despite the strong misgivings of Canning and others, in January 1845 Lord Aberdeen recommended Nesselrode's proposal as a basis for a final settlement of the Muhammara boundary.[23] The delimitation was recommended to the Porte in a joint Anglo–Russian representation of March 1845. After initially rejecting the proposal, the Porte eventually agreed to this arrangement in an official note of 1 March 1846, provided that this would not "affect the Porte's right of property to the river, the course of which was still to belong wholly and exclusively to the Porte, which only granted freedom of passage to Persian vessels".[24]

The draft and final treaties of Erzerum, November 1846 and May 1847

The mediating commissioners drew up a nine-article draft treaty in November 1846. Article 2, dealing with Muhammara and the Shatt al-Arab, incorporated Nesselrode's delimitation proposal and stipulated that the Ottomans agree to cede to Persia the city, port and anchorage of Muhammara and also the island of Khizr.[25] The draft treaty survived with no modifications to constitute the document eventually signed on 31 May 1847 by the Persians, the Ottomans and the two mediating powers at Erzerum.[26] A series of strict Ottoman demands had to be satisfied before the Erzerum treaty was signed. In addition, the mediating powers felt it prudent to keep the Persians in the dark as far as the details of these assurances were concerned.[27]

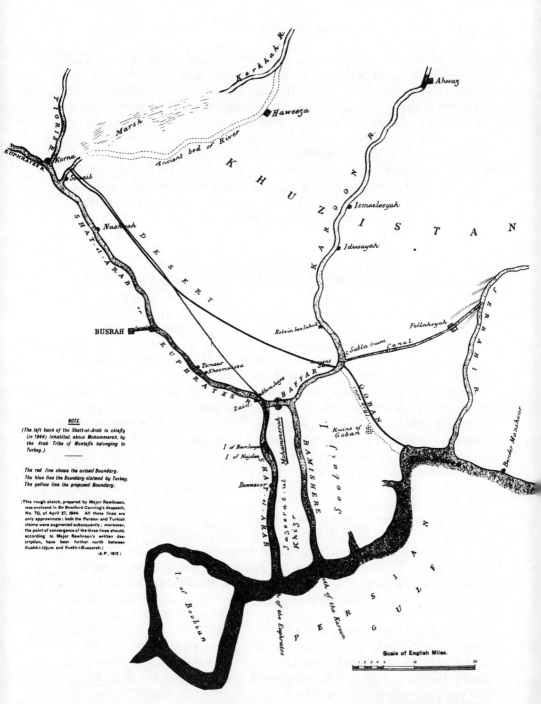

Scale of English Miles.

Figure 7.1 Rawlinson's proposal for a boundary in the Muhammara region, 1844. The middle line, bisecting the respective claims of Persia (to the left) and the Ottoman Empire (to the right) and running through the middle of Khizr (Abadan) Island, was recommended by Major Rawlinson in his memorandum of January 1844 and adopted by Sir Stratford Canning in his representations to Russia during summer 1844 (taken from IOLR file: L/P&S/10/266).

The explanatory notes issued to the Ottoman Porte by the
mediating powers, April 1847 and March 1848 and the
difficulties caused by the ratification of the Erzerum treaty

After earlier assurances had failed to satisfy Ottoman demands, a joint Anglo–Russian note of April 1847 finally assured the Porte, without saying so explicitly, that its full sovereignty over the Shatt al-Arab was incontrovertible. The note specified that: "in ceding to Persia the city, port and anchorage of Muhammara and the island of Khizr, the Sublime Porte was not ceding any other parts there may be in this region".[28]

It is worth noting that support for Nesselrode's proposed east bank boundary delimitation had been by no means uniform in Britain and Russia in the period leading up to the Erzerum treaty's signature. In a letter of 3 March 1847, Lord Palmerston, who was at various stages both prime minister and foreign secretary, made even stronger reservations about granting the Porte the assurances they required concerning sovereignty over the Shatt al-Arab:

I have to state to you with reference to the pretension which has been advanced by the Porte to an absolute right of sovereignty over the Chat el-Arab, that when the opposite banks of a river belong as they will do in the case of the lower portion of the Chat el-Arab, to differing Powers, it would be contrary to International usage to give to one of the two powers the exclusive sovereignty of that portion of the course of such River, and that therefore this proposal of the Turkish Government's seems to be inadmissible.[29]

Nevertheless, the Ottomans felt reasonably assured after the issue of the joint Anglo–Russian note of 14 April 1847 that their sovereignty over the whole Shatt al-Arab waterway would not be open to question. To judge by the line laid down by Colonel Williams on 4 February 1850, it can only be assumed that Britain intended this to be so, irrespective of Palmerston's initial views. In any case it was a much more pragmatic Palmerston who conceded, on 11 October 1851, that "the boundary between Turkey and Persia can never finally be settled except by an arbitrary decision on the part of Great Britain and Russia".[30]

The Persian plenipotentiary Mirza Takki signed the Erzerum treaty oblivious to the issue of the note of 14 April 1847 delivered by the mediating commissioners to the Porte. Yet, when the treaty came up for ratification, annexed to it was the same note. Britain and Russia hoped that Mirza Takki would feel obliged to endorse the assurances given to the Porte. After consistently refusing to do so, in a note of 19 January 1848 the Persian representative formally acceded to the contents of the explanatory note but stated that this action had been taken only as a short-term measure to prevent the failure of negotiations and that he had possessed no real authority to make the required endorsement.[31] Nevertheless, ratifications of the Erzerum treaty and the attached explanatory note were exchanged between Persia and the Ottoman empire on 21 March 1848 but not before a further joint Anglo–Russian note had been issued to the Porte, formalizing and reinforcing all the assurances previously delivered.[32]

The Williams line of February 1850

Article 3 of the 1847 Erzerum treaty had stipulated the appointment of a four power boundary commission whose task was to determine conclusively the precise delimitation of the boundary between the two states.[33] After innumerable delays, in January 1850 the commission commenced operations at Muhammara.[34] It soon became clear that the ratification of the 1847 treaty and the explanatory note had failed to solve the Perso–Ottoman dispute over the limits of territorial control at the head of the Persian Gulf. The Ottoman commissioner, Dervish Pasha, manipulated the wording of the explanatory note to advance a territorial claim deep into Persian Khuzistan, recognizing the walled port of Muhammara and the island of Khizr – now established indisputably under Persian sovereignty – only as enclaves within long-established Ottoman territory (Fig. 7.2). Persia responded to the Porte's exorbitant demands by interpreting the explanatory note to have recognized its sovereignty over the east bank of the Shatt al-Arab from its confluence with the Jaab river, just south of Qurnah, down stream to the Persian Gulf.[35] The precise line claimed ran southwest from Hawizah along the south bank of the Jaab and then along the middle of the Shatt al-Arab throughout its course south of this point (Fig. 7.2).

If the boundary delimitation prescribed by the 1847 treaty and its annex had been vague concerning the river down stream of Muhammara, then it was less clear still for the section up stream of the port. Thus, shortly after the Ottomans and Persians had submitted their interpretations of the April 1847 explanatory note, Colonel Williams proposed a line on 4 February 1850 that, it was maintained, reflected as accurately as possible the delimitation implied in the 1847 treaty and the explanatory note (Fig. 7.2).[36] Bisecting the extravagant claims put forward by the Persian and Ottoman plenipotentiaries, the line ran southwards from Hawizah to the junction of the Jideyeh canal with the Shatt al-Arab and from there along the east bank of the river down stream to the Persian Gulf. The governments of the mediating powers soon pronounced themselves in favour of Williams' award.[37]

In March 1850 Persia communicated its response to Colonel Williams' proposal.[38] While seemingly prepared to abandon any pretensions to sovereignty over the Shatt al-Arab waters, Persia insisted on a delimitation that left the river at a point 6½ kilometres further up stream than had Williams' proposal. This small stretch of territory was claimed by Persia since it was populated by Ka'b tribesmen; the mediating powers argued against Persian control of this section, however, as this could pose a strategic threat to the Ottoman port of Basra. Colonel Sheil, British minister in Tehran, finally persuaded Persia to accept the delimitation prescribed by Williams on 25

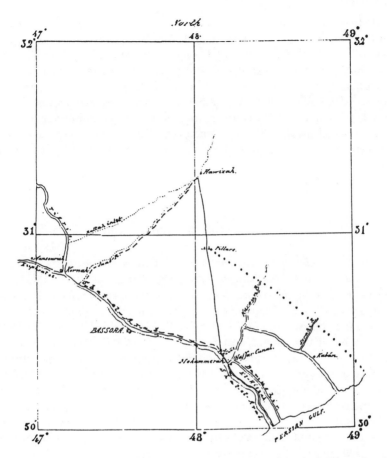

Figure 7.2 The Williams line, 1850. This copy of an original hand-drawn map shows (as an unbroken line) Colonel Williams's award of February 1850. The dashed pencil line has been added to illustrate the Persian Commissioner's claim of January 1850. The dotted pencil line has been added to illustrate the Ottoman Commissioner's claim of January 1850. (Taken from FO 78/2719)

May 1850. Persia accepted this only on the condition that the Ka'b tribesmen remaining northwest of the Williams line were transferred to Persian territory.[39] Conversely, the Porte categorically rejected the Williams line. The mediating commissioners then tried to secure the agreement of the Persians and Ottomans to respect the Williams line temporarily, on a *status quo* basis. After protracted difficulties the Persian and Ottoman commissioners provisionally accepted in writing the *status quo* at Muhammara as defined by the Williams line.[40]

This was the last development of note in the mid-19th century. The dispute over the Shatt al-Arab boundary did not recur until the first decade of the 20th century. Incidentally, it was not until September 1952 that Williams reported the completion of the survey of the Perso/Ottoman border zone from the Persian Gulf to Mount Ararat. The British and the Russian commissioner, Colonel Tchirikov, had long since limited their ambitions to establishing the area of disputed territory along the border rather than precisely delimiting any line. Williams, a fastidious note-keeper, intended to produce a detailed report of the commission's activities on his return to London but, incredibly, all of his notes, memoranda and other correspondence (much of which dealt with Muhammara and presumably the basis of his line) were lost to the Thames near Gravesend at the end of the voyage home.[41]

The evolution of the Shatt al-Arab boundary, 1908–13

The Shaikh of Muhammara's fears of Ottoman encroachment across the southern Perso/Ottoman boundary in 1908

The Shaikh of Muhammara (successor to the semi-autonomous Ka'b dynasty in Muhammara) had exaggerated perceptions in 1908 of an imminent Ottoman threat to his autonomous control of Persian territory east of the Shatt al-Arab, which led ultimately to a debate between the Foreign Office and the India Office over the precise status and alignment of the Perso/Ottoman boundary in its southern reaches.[42] His concern prompted Sir N. O'Conor, British ambassador in Constantinople, to draft a note of remonstration to the Porte, the contents of which were never officially communicated as the danger from the Ottomans proved illusory. Importantly, however, O'Conor received the following directives from British Foreign Secretary Sir Edward Grey in a despatch of 25 February 1908:

> In this district [Muhammara] His Majesty's Government are not prepared to recognise any other frontier than that laid down by the mediating commissioners in 1850.[43]

Lieutenant Wilson's findings of May 1909

Yet only a year later, in May 1909, Lieutenant A. T. Wilson, British Consul at Muhammara, pointed out that the boundary recommended by Colonel Williams in February 1850 differed considerably from the frontier recognized locally by the Muhammara and Basra authorities (Fig. 7.3).[44] The boundary, as locally recognized in 1909, ran down the centre and not the east bank of the Shatt al-Arab, while the land boundary left the east bank of the river at a point some 10 kilometres further up stream from the point indicated by the mediating commissioners in 1850. Wilson went on to suggest that the British government should disregard the 1850 Williams line and simply take their stand on a subsequent Anglo–Russian Declaration allegedly made in 1865 whereby the whole Perso/Ottoman boundary was to be found within the limits of the frontier zone as indicated on the "Carte Identique" of 1869.[45] The "Carte Identique", drawn up by the mediating powers to incorporate the findings of the Mixed Delimitation Commission, which surveyed the boundary between 1850 and 1852, depicted a boundary zone that averaged 40 kilometres in width.[46]

Wilson concluded that his proposition would "perpetuate the *status quo*, as is presumably desired by His Majesty's Government".[47] In brief, the maintenance of the *status quo* was deemed important for two reasons. First, to adhere rigidly to the 1850 Williams line and ignore the locally observed line would throw the palace, court house and prison of the Shaikh of Muhammara into Ottoman territory. This would be inimical to the well established Government of India policy of close support for the shaikh, which had been actively propounded by the British authorities in the Persian Gulf for the previous decade. In 1899, Colonel Meade, Political Resident in the Persian Gulf, had informed the shaikh that the British authorities considered him to be the most influential person in those parts and that they intended as far as possible to support and maintain his strong position.[48] Secondly, Wilson was concerned not to disturb unduly Britain's fast-developing commercial interests in the Muhammara and Khuzistan region. The Knox D'Arcy venture had discovered oil in commercial quantities near Masjid-i-Sulaiman in 1908 and it was soon apparent that Muhammara's existing landing facilities on both banks of the Karun between the river's junction with the Shatt al-Arab and Muhammara town proper farther east were woefully inadequate for the large increase in river traffic anticipated following the oil find.[49] Only landing facilities on the Shatt al-Arab itself could accommodate the large ocean-going steamers that were required to import bulky drilling equipment for the nascent oil industry in southwest Persia. Political Resident Sir Percy Cox admitted during the summer of 1912 that with the projected incorporation of Muhammara into the Persian railroad system, the transfer of landing wharves from the Karun to the east bank of the Shatt al-Arab was not just desirable but inevitable.[50] Such a move, when completed, would mean that both Muhammara's landing and anchorage facilities would lie on or within the Shatt al-Arab and that both features, if the 1850 Williams line was to be adopted in its entirety, would technically be subject to Ottoman jurisdiction. All of this must have weighed heavily in Wilson's thinking. It should be noted that Muhammara's midstream anchorage in the Shatt al-Arab had been used ever since Muhammara and the lower course of the river had been opened up to steamship navigation during the last third of the 19th century.[51]

British Secretary for Foreign Affairs, Sir Edward Grey, responded to Wilson's "zonal" argument by stating that, while the Foreign Office had no desire to disturb the *status quo* as observed locally, the validity of the 1850 Williams line still held.[52]

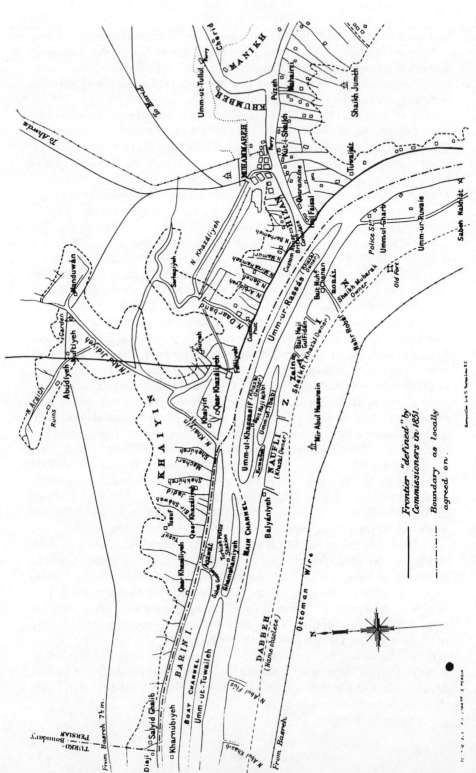

Figure 7.3 The locally recognized boundary, 1909. The map shows the frontier as locally observed by Lieutenant Wilson in

The exchanges between the India Office and the
Foreign Office on the Muhammara boundary, 1910–12

In the spring of 1910 Cox lent further support to Wilson's findings. Rather than recommending that the southern Perso/Ottoman boundary be redrawn within the frontier zone, as Wilson had done, Cox proposed that the Williams line of 1850 be disregarded altogether and that the locally recognized boundary be adopted.[53] He stressed that the strict observance of the 1850 line would throw the palace, court house and the prison of the Shaikh of Muhammara into Ottoman territory, while to confirm Ottoman sovereignty over the Shatt al-Arab would deprive Persia of two important islands attached to Khizr island at low tide.

The contents of Cox's memorandum were slowly digested during the latter half of 1910 as the Foreign Office began to address the question of how it might best develop a Shatt al-Arab policy that categorically refuted neither the 1850 Williams line nor the locally recognized boundary first highlighted by Wilson in 1909. During this period Whitehall issued reassuring words in turn to the Shaikh of Muhammara, the Porte and the India Office without coming down firmly on the side of any one of them. Importantly, however, the Foreign Office maintained that the Williams line of 1850 should be retained as the basis of all discussion on the subject.[54] The attitude of the Foreign Office hardened somewhat during 1911. It was now considered impossible to disregard the decisions taken by the Delimitation Commission in 1850, whatever the present *de facto* line might be, since the "zonal" findings of the commission were directly or indirectly the sole protection for the interests of the Persian government on other parts of the frontier.

The India Office, meanwhile, continued to support the argument for British recognition of the Muhammara frontier as locally observed in 1909. In June 1911 Lord Crewe stated: "by their recognition of the line proposed in 1850 they [the Porte] have allowed a situation to grow for sixty years in which the mid-channel [of the Shatt al-Arab] has, without challenge, been accepted by local usage".[55] As late as May 1912 Cox presented further evidence: "the local Turkish authorities have accorded unequivocal and repeated recognition of the present boundary by the erection of marks and the maintenance for many years of a permanent frontier customs post at Diaji".[56]

The Parker memorandum of April 1912

Crucial to the future course of the dispute was the publication in April 1912 of a Foreign Office memorandum on the Muhammara dispute by Alwyn Parker.[57] The arguments in favour of adopting the boundary as locally recognized were examined in great detail. In early 1912 it seemed likely that the Perso/Ottoman frontier dispute might be forwarded to the International Court of Arbitration in The Hague, in accordance with the clauses of the December 1911 Tehran Protocol, signed by Persia and the Ottoman empire.

Parker suggested that the arguments for disregarding the Williams line of 1850 would be unlikely to prevail before the court unless it could be convincingly demonstrated that the mediating powers had, in 1850–1, misinterpreted the express terms of the 1847 treaty and the annexed explanatory note. Parker largely dismissed the arguments for a mid-channel delimitation in the Shatt al-Arab, finally concluding that this would directly contravene Article 2 of the Erzerum treaty. In reaching this judgement he relied heavily on the legal principle of *expressum facit cessare tacitum*. In other words, Parker in effect supported the Ottoman argument of the time that, by specifying only rights of navigation for Persian vessels, the 1847 treaty implicitly denied Persia all other rights. He added that Britain stood to gain nothing from a mid-channel Shatt al-Arab delimitation and that the only consideration that could be urged for such a line was that the Bahmanshir Channel was no longer navigable. In sum it was concluded that Britain should insist on the Williams line of 1850 as a general basis of negotiation and the strict observance of that line from the Persian Gulf to Failieh, thus making the frontier the left bank along Khizr island and not the mid-channel of the Shatt al-Arab. Parker suggested a modification of the line at Failieh to include an additional 10½ kilometres of upstream territory on the east bank of the Shatt so as to incorporate the boundary as observed locally, thereby including the Shaikh of Muhammara's palace, court house and prison within Persian territory.[58]

As has been mentioned, Parker concluded that "British interests have nothing to gain from pressing the argument *medium filum aquae*".[59] It is unclear whether Parker was aware of the potentially vulnerable position of Muhammara's anchorage facilities in the mid-stream of the Shatt al-Arab. He certainly failed to address the issue in his lengthy memorandum and made no recommendation that the boundary be adjusted to the median line of the Shatt opposite the port. In July 1912, however, just one week before Sir Edward Grey announced his ultimately successful compromise solution for the Shatt question, Parker enquired of the India Office the exact position of Muhammara's existing anchorage in the mid-stream of the Shatt al-Arab.[60] Sir Percy Cox hurriedly replied that it extended along the Shatt mid-stream 4,000 metres up stream from the junction with the Karun and 1,000 metres down stream. Continuing to argue for the locally recognized boundary along the mid-stream first recognized by Wilson in 1909 or at the very least the portion of the river alongside Muhammara, Cox noted that, if mooring buoys were provided, all ships moored at the anchorage could be berthed on the Persian side of the mid-stream channel line.[61]

Sir Edward Grey's compromise solution of July 1912
In his important memorandum dated 18 July 1912, Sir Edward Grey proposed a compromise boundary delimitation for Muhammara and the Shatt al-Arab, which was later confirmed in the 29 July 1913 Anglo–Turkish

Declaration fixing the Perso/Ottoman boundary from Hawizah to the Persian Gulf.[62] In turn this alignment was embodied in the 17 November 1913 Constantinople Protocol, which settled the whole length of the Perso–Ottoman boundary (Fig. 7.4). Essentially following Parker's recommendations, Grey took the viewpoint that if the articles of any new boundary agreement were to be based solely upon the clauses of the 1847 Treaty of Erzerum then nothing more could be claimed in principle for Persia than freedom of navigation within the Shatt al-Arab. Yet Grey was fully aware, as we shall see below, that the Erzerum treaty had said nothing in itself concerning sovereignty of the river. Grey proposed that the 1850 Williams line should continue to constitute the boundary line in principle, but that the locally observed line should be urged to accommodate genuine Persian grievances and Muhammara's commercial needs. Therefore, after Parker's suggestion, the Shatt al-Arab frontier was extended 10½ kilometres up stream from Failieh and, further to Parker's suggestions, the boundary delimitation was extended to the median line of the river opposite Muhammara, so that Persia might possess jurisdiction over the existing anchorage and the envisaged landing facilities within and along the Shatt al-Arab. Jurisdiction would also be gained over the Karun bar. The islands in the Shatt al-Arab that were attached to Khizr (Abadan) island at low tide were transferred to Persian sovereignty.[63]

Although Grey had relied heavily on Parker's findings, largely adopting his suggested delimitation (save for the Muhammara adjustment), some of his observations seemed strangely at odds with the Parker memorandum. Parker had concluded that Lieutenant Wilson's proposal for a mid-channel delimitation would, if implemented, contravene the Treaty of Erzerum. Yet Grey stated in his memorandum that:

> The records of the past 300 years . . . are far from supporting any claim on the part of Turkey to "prior occupancy and long undisturbed possession" of the Shatt-el-Arab; while no express stipulation is contained in the Treaty of Erzerum as to the ownership if the river.
>
> If, therefore, His Majesty's Government had strict regard either to purely local considerations or to the letter of the treaties they would not hesitate to press for the frontier as locally recognised along its whole length from Hawizeh to the Persian Gulf.[64]

Grey then went on to explain the reasons that lay behind his adoption, for the most part, of the delimitation suggested earlier in the year by Parker for the Shatt al-Arab:

> they [HMG] prefer to look at the negotiations in which they are now engaged as a whole, and are sincerely anxious to arrive at an arrange ment which both parties can accept *ex animo*, and which, by removing all parts of grievance and friction not only between themselves, but also between the Sublime Porte and the Sheikh of Mohammerah, will place the relations of all concerned on a thoroughly satisfactory foot-

ing. Provided therefore the Turkish Government will accept the frontier *status quo* [i.e the locally recognized frontier first observed by Wilson] from the neighbourhood of Hawizeh to the point where the Khaiyin Canal and the Nahr Nazaileh enter the Shatt al-Arab, then His Majesty's Government are prepared to use their influence with the Persian Government and the Shaikh of Muhammara to induce them to recognise Turkish sovereignty over the whole waterway of the Shatt al-Arab [subject to the exceptions mentioned earlier].[65]

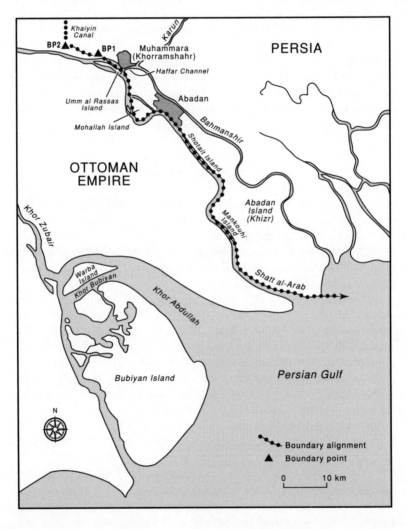

Figure 7.4 Grey's compromise proposal, 1912; embodied in the Constantinople Protocol, 1913.

In spite of Grey's observations on the 1847 treaty and ownership of the Shatt al-Arab, the Foreign Office informed the Persian government only one and a half years later that the Erzerum treaty with its explanatory note had established Ottoman sovereignty over the river. In December 1913, following the signature of the Constantinople Protocol, Persia complained that instructions despatched from Tehran to ensure that Persia's "well established sovereign rights on the Shatt al-Arab" were maintained did not reach Constantinople in time for the signature of the Protocol. The Foreign Office rejected this proposition out of hand, stating that Persian rights of sovereignty over the river were non-existent, as was clear from the wording of Article 2 of the Erzerum treaty and the acceptance by Persia of the Williams line of 1850.[66]

Grey's overriding objective in nominating his proposal of July 1912 seemed to have been to come to an arrangement from which both Persia and the Porte could be seen to have demonstrably gained. Grey was not blind to the manipulative worth of his compromise. In its dealings with the Porte, Britain could highlight the locally recognized boundary along the mid-channel of the Shatt al-Arab so as to underline that, in any future proposal confirming Ottoman sovereignty over the river, a large concession was being made to the Porte. Yet in August 1912, when Grey's proposals were communicated to the Persian government it was stressed that the Muhammara proposal and certain adjustments in the northern stretch of the border zone, with which the Russians were primarily concerned, were valuable gains for Persia for which it might have to pay in other sections, for example Zohab.[67] It is also important to note that, in August 1912, the Persian government also communicated its unconditional acceptance of the explanatory notes issued in April 1847 and March 1848 by the mediating powers to the Ottoman Porte.[68]

Concluding remarks

Both the Williams line of February 1850 and Sir Edward Grey's proposal of July 1912 were compromises, yet each was made for different reasons. The Williams line seems, for the most part, to have been an honest attempt by the mediating powers to interpret the express terms of the 1847 Treaty of Erzerum and its explanatory notes after the corroboration of local features on the ground. Grey's proposal was a compromise between the boundary as locally recognized in the first decade of the 20th century and the Williams line of 1850 and seemed above all to be governed by expediency, the need to highlight that both the Ottomans and the Persians were gaining, or at least losing nothing, in his award. Grey also needed to view any proposal for this section of the frontier as part of a much wider settlement of the whole Perso/Ottoman boundary.

It is clear that right up until Grey's compromise boundary delimitation was decided upon, utter confusion reigned about what should properly constitute the boundary along the Shatt al-Arab and, more specifically, what alignment had been introduced by the express terms of the 1847 treaty. This was an inevitable consequence of a treaty that supposedly introduced an international river boundary yet made no mention of the sovereignty of that river. Luckily, succeeding protocols and treaties signed in Constantinople (1913), Tehran (1937) and Algiers (1975) committed each side to an unequivocal statement of where the boundary lay. It is nonetheless noteworthy that the first two of these three instruments assumed that the 1847 treaty with its explanatory notes had set a Perso/Ottoman boundary along the east bank of the Shatt al-Arab. This remains the conventional interpretation. The situation was, however, much more ambiguous and untidy than most observers can possibly imagine.

Notes

1. R. N. Schofield, *Kuwait and Iraq: historical claims and territorial disputes* (London: Royal Institute of International Affairs, 1991; 2nd edn, 1993).
2. G. Biger, "The lacustrine and riverine boundaries of Israel: the Sea of Galilee, River Jordan and Red Sea", in *World boundaries: the Middle East and North Africa*, C. H. Schofield & R. N. Schofield (eds), 100–110 (London: Routledge, 1994).
3. R. N. Schofield, *Evolution of the Shatt al-Arab boundary dispute*, 36–7 (Wisbech: Menas Press, 1986).
4. See K. McLachlan, Chapter 6.
5. G. E. Hubbard, *From the Gulf to Ararat*, 2 (Edinburgh: William Blackwood, 1916).
6. Schofield & Schofield, op. cit.
7. Schofield, op. cit. (1986), 49–50.
8. J. R. V. Prescott, *Boundaries and frontiers*, 39–48 (London: Croom Helm, 1978).
9. M. Khadduri, *The Gulf war: the origins and implications of the Iraq–Iran conflict*, 34 (New York: Oxford University Press, 1988).
10. R. M. Burrell & K. S. McLachlan, "The political geography of the Persian Gulf states", in *The Persian Gulf states*, A. J. Cottrell (ed.), 122 (Baltimore: Johns Hopkins University Press, 1979).
11. D. Pipes, "A border adrift: origins of the conflict", in *The Iran–Iraq war: new weapons, old conflicts*, S. Tahir-Kheli & S. Ayubi (eds), 13–14 (New York: Praeger, 1983).
12. M. C. Niebuhr, *Travels through Arabia, and other countries in the east*, vol. 2, 150 (Edinburgh, 1792), English translation by R. Heron. Originally published as *Reisebeschreibung nach Arabien und andern umliegenden Ländern* (Copenhagen, 1772).
13. M. al-Najjar & N. F. Safwat, "Arab sovereignty over the Shatt al-Arab during the Kaabide period", in *The Iran-Iraq war*, M. S. El-Azhary (ed.), 20–1 (London: Croom Helm, 1984).
14. Schofield, op. cit. (1986), 23–4.
15. R. N. Schofield, "The shaping of British policy towards the Shatt al-Arab question, 1843-1934", in *International boundaries and boundary conflict resolution*, C. E. R. Grundy-Warr (ed.), 324–8 (Proceedings of the 1989 IBRU conference, University of Durham, 1990).

16. A. Melamid, "The Shatt al-Arab boundary dispute", *The Middle East Journal* **22** (1968), 351-7.

17. Foreign Office, Extracts from Foreign Office correspondence relative to the Turco-Persian boundary negotiations, Part I: 1843-4, April 1912. FO 881/10024.

18. Major Rawlinson, "Memorandum on the subject of Mohammerah and the Shaab tribe", 6 January 1844. FO 881/10038.

19. W. F. Williams to Sir Stratford Canning, 15 October 1843. FO 881/10008.

20. Rawlinson, op. cit., 6 January 1844.

21. Extracts from Foreign Office correspondence, 1843-4, April 1912.

22. Count Nesselrode, "Memorandum communicated when in attendance of the Emperor Nicholas I on the occasion of His Majesty's visit to England", September 1844. FO 881/10039.

23. Lord Aberdeen to Sir Stratford Canning, 7 January 1845. FO 881/10038.

24. Rechid Pacha, "Traduction d'une Note officiale [sic] remise par son Excellence Rechid Pacha à Sir Stratford Canning", 1 March 1846. FO 881/10041.

25. H. Wellesley (later Lord Cowley) to Lord Palmerston, 3 November 1846. FO 78/2715.

26. Foreign Office, Translation of the 31 May 1847 Treaty of Erzurum, 1 June 1847. FO 881/10041.

27. Lord Cowley to Lord Palmerston, 15 June 1847. FO 78/2716.

28. Foreign Office, op. cit., 1 June 1847.

29. Lord Palmerston to Lord Bloomfield, 3 March 1847. FO 78/2716.

30. Lord Palmerston to Sir G. H. Seymour, 11 October 1851. FO 78/2721.

31. Mirza Muhammad Khan to Lord Cowley, 19 January 1848. FO 881/10041.

32. Lord Cowley to Lord Palmerston, 21 March 1848. FO 78/2717.

33. Foreign Office, op. cit., 1 June 1847.

34. Foreign Office, "Journaux des conférences des quatres commissaires pour la délimitation de la frontière turco-persane", 16 January – 5 February 1850. FO 881/10041.

35. Colonel Sheil to Sir Stratford Canning, 25 March 1850. FO 78/2719.

36. W. F. Williams to Sir Stratford Canning, 4 February 1850. FO 78/2719.

37. Sir Stratford Canning to Lord Palmerston, 30 May 1850. FO 78/2719.

38. Sheil, op. cit., 25 March 1850.

39. Canning, op. cit., 30 May 1850.

40. Sir Stratford Canning to Lord Palmerston, 31 December 1851. FO 881/10041.

41. R. N. Schofield, *The Iran–Iraq border, 1840–1958*, vol. II, xv (Farnham Common, England: Archive Editions, 1989).

42. E. Parkes, "Memorandum relative to the British assurances given to the Shaykh of Muhammara in 1899 and 1902-10", 12 May 1912, FO 881/10039.

43. Foreign Office, "Supplementary memorandum respecting Mohammerah", 4 March 1908. FO 416/35.

44. Sir Arnold Wilson to Mr G. Barclay, 26 May 1909. FO 371/710.

45. Ibid.

46. C. H. D. Ryder, "The demarcation of the Turco–Persian boundary in 1913-14", *Geographical Journal* **66** (1925), 228.

47. Wilson, op. cit., 26 May 1909.

48. Parkes, op. cit., 12 May 1912.

49. Schofield, op. cit. (1986), 47-8.

50. Sir Percy Cox to India Office, 15 July 1912. L/P&S/10/266.

51. Ibid.

52. Sir Edward Grey to Sir G. Barclay, 27 October 1909. FO 371/710.

53. Sir Percy Cox to Sir Edward Grey, 8 May 1910. FO 371/948.

54. A. Parker, "Memorandum respecting the points raised by Lieutenant-Colonel Cox in his despatch of 7 August 1910 on the Turco–Persian frontier question", 5 September 1910. FO 371/949.
55. Lord Crewe, India Office to Foreign Office, 3 June 1911. FO 371/1179.
56. Sir Percy Cox to Mr A. Parker, 23 May 1912. L/P&S/10/266.
57. A. Parker, "Memorandum respecting the frontier between Muhammara and Turkey", 3 April 1912. FO 881/14638.
58. Ibid.
59. Ibid.
60. Mr A. Parker to Mr A. Hirtzel, India Office, 9 July 1912. L/P&S/10/266.
61. Cox, op. cit., 15 July 1912.
62. Sir Edward Grey to Sir G. Buchanan, 18 July 1912. L/P&S/10/266.
63. Ibid.
64. Ibid.
65. Ibid.
66. Foreign Office, "Memorandum on the frontier between Persia and Turkey and Persia and Iraq, 1639–1934", 8 January 1935. Foreign Office confidential print No. 14514.
67. Sir Walter Townley to Sir Edward Grey, 30 August 1912. L/P&S/10/266.
68. H. Shipley, "Report on the Turco–Persian frontier commission of 1912", 19 March 1913. FO 881/12714.

CHAPTER EIGHT
Ethno-linguistic links between southern Iraq and Khuzistan

BRUCE INGHAM

At the head of the Gulf the linguistic boundary between Arabic and the Iranian dialects does not in fact correspond with the fairly well established political boundary. The latter goes up the Shatt al-Arab to just above Khor-ramshahr on the Persian side opposite Abu Khasib on the Iraqi side and then generally northwards across the plain, keeping about 15–30 kilometres to the east of the Tigris until it reaches the foothills of the Zagros range, where it follows the line of the mountains in a northwesterly direction, as shown in Fig. 8.1. The linguistic boundary, in contrast, crosses this on a northwesterly axis, with Arabic being spoken on the plain and Iranian dialects (in which I include Kurdish) on the high ground. Thus we have Arabic-speaking populations in Iran and Kurdish-speaking populations in Iraq. In the southern Persian region of Khuzistan the native population is uniformly Arabic, although the growth of the oil industry resulted in substantial immigration from the Persian-speaking areas to the oil towns of Abadan and Ahwaz. Ironically also the Iraqi invasion of Khuzistan, which had mistakenly expected Khuzistani Arab support, resulted in considerable displacement of the Arab population to the more northern cities.

Linguistic geography of southern Iraq and Khuzistan

The area of southern Iraq up to Samawah on the Euphrates and Kut on the Tigris and the plain of Khuzistan can be regarded as culturally and linguistically if not a unit at least part of a discernible continuum. It is possible to point to cultural features such as the prevalence of Shi'ite Islam and the presence of the Arabic language throughout the area, which is generally well known. If however we examine the dialect geography of the region we note that the isoglosses (lines dividing different variants of a linguistic unit) do not divide the area into an eastern and western block, i.e. along the present political boundary, but rather divide into areas relatable to water, i.e. at the river mouth, down river, up river, in the marshlands, away from the

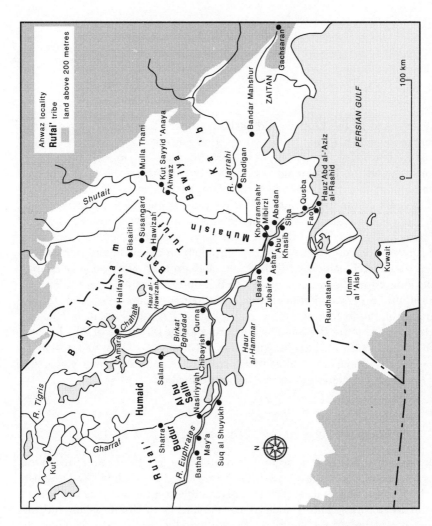

Figure 8.1 Map showing southern Iraq and Khuzistan: localities and tribes.

marshlands, etc. These do not of course divide it in any way visible except to the linguist, and even to the linguist the picture presented is not so much a division into discrete areas, as a continuum or spectrum of different types centred on the Shatt al-Arab and Karun rivers and fanning out northwards. The linguistic areas that can be perceived, again with a fair degree of gross generalization, are the following:

- The Shatt al-Arab and lower Karun and parts of the Euphrates below Nasiriyyah and the banks of the Jarrahi around Shadigan including the main old towns of the region, i.e. Basra and Khorramshahr.
- The marshlands of the Haur al-Hawizah and the Haur al-Hammar, which centre on the junction of the Tigris and Euphrates and on the Tigris in the area of Amarah and across into Persian territory.
- The *badiyah* or open country between the rivers embracing also some of the newer towns such as Ahwaz.
- Zubair to the southwest of Basra.

The above conforms to a fairly well observed fact about linguistic geography, namely that rivers form the centres of linguistic regions rather than dividing them;[1] thus it would be unnatural to find that the Shatt al-Arab constituted a linguistic boundary. The above linguistic grouping is based on many different features, which have been examined in detail elsewhere.[2]

However, Figure 8.2 gives an illustration of this by the distribution of the reflexes of the classical arabic *jim* in the area. Here one can see that in the central marshland areas of the Haur al-Hammar and Haur al-Hawizah the reflex is [ž] like the French [j], while in most of the rest of the southern river network the reflex is [y]. North of this and to the west of the Euphrates the reflex is the more usual [j], which links it up with the rest of central Arabia. The reflex [y] incidentally is continued down the Gulf settlements and found in Kuwait, Bahrain, Qatar and the Emirates. One sees therefore that the southern part of the river network forms a definite linguistic area distinguished from those outside it, with the marshlands forming a sub-area within it.

This linguistic configuration can be correlated with wide political–tribal groupings discernible in the recent history, and shown in Fig. 8.1. First, the core of the Shatt al-Arab and associated rivers forms the economic power base of the Ka'b. The history of the Ka'b in Khuzistan can be traced back to the Safavi period when a family of Sayyids from Mecca, chieftains of Wasit in southern Iraq, became Walis of Hawizah in Khuzistan in southwest Persia. This ushered in an era of Arab domination of the area. At the end of the 17th century the Arab tribe of the Bani Ka'b (often referred to as the Chaub) moved into Khuzistan and took over the area from the Afshar Turks, becoming clients of the Wali of Hawizah and later themselves becoming rulers of the area. Layard, who visited the area in the 1800s,[3] mentions that many refugees from the principal towns in the province had settled within the territories of the Arab tribes[4] and that it had become a common place of refuge for political offenders. He also mentions, speaking

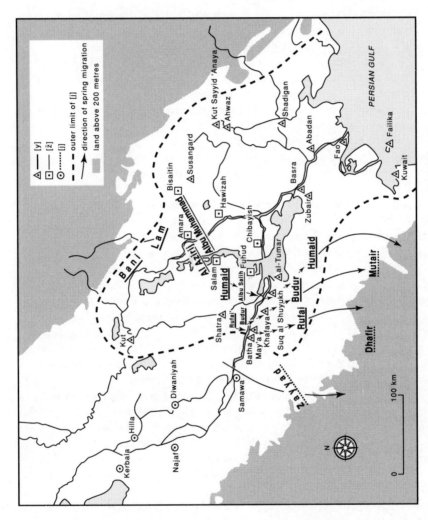

Figure 8.2 Map showing lingusitic geography of southern Iraq and Khuzistan.

of Shushter, that "the Arab language is generally understood, although the Persian prevails, and the Arabic dress is at the same time affected in preference to that of the Persian".[5] We thus see a picture of what seems to be a quite prosperous area in which a gradual Arabization of elements of the Persian population was taking place, in which language and dress are relevant features. De Bode, visiting Shush in the early 19th century, remarks on the dress and prosperity of the Arabs of the region:

> The white turbans negligently twisted around the heads of the men contrasted boldly with their dark complexions and jet black hair . . . while their broad striped abbas, or cloaks hung loosely on their shoulders in plaits. These Arabs appeared to be more opulent or at least more attentive to their dress, than the generality of the Iliyat tribes of Persia.[6]

Another traveller, Stocqueler, refers to the clothing of the Chaub in some detail:

> The costume of the Chabeans is like their language – a mixture. They wear the Persian kabah, or green tunic, loose trousers and slippers, the cummer, or girdle, and a lilac cloth turban of the same form as the Arab's. The sheikhs wear crimson and gold dresses on extraordinary occasions, but for ordinary use content themselves with crimson chintz, variegated with yellow flowers in imitation of gold.[7]

This is interesting in showing the interaction of Persian and Arab culture in the area. The Ka'b seem to have been independent of the rule of Basra at most times and had settlements initially at Guban at the head of Khor Musa until 1747 and then later at Shadigan (or Fallahiyyah, to give it its Arabic name). The later rule of the Muhaisin under Shaikh Khazal in the late 19th and early 20th centuries moved the seat of power to Muhammara (Khorramshahr) on the lower Karun. The Ka'b and Muhaisin of today speak an Arabic dialect closely linked to that of the Shatt al-Arab region differentiated mainly by the number of Persian words they use, and would seem to have usually been involved in one way or another in the Persian sphere of influence, but also to have constituted a strong independent sea-borne power that fought successive foreign powers including the Portuguese, the Turks and the British, and occasionally exacted tribute from Kuwaiti vessels in the 18th century.[8]

Secondly, the marshland area of the Haur al-Hawizah and its hinterland equally forms a dialect area spanning the Iran/Iraq boundary that may be linked to the previous prosperity of the area under the Walis of Hawizah (the Musha'sha'iyyah as they are locally remembered), which, it is popularly supposed, was ruined overnight by the collapse of the great dyke at Kut Nahr Hashim on the Karkhah in 1832[9] or 1837,[10] which left the agricultural land high and dry and turned much of the rest into swamp. Thirdly, the *badiyah* of Khuzistan seems to have been easily open to encroachment from the west and forms a link with Bedouin or Arab (sheep-herding nomad) tribes from the Euphrates and beyond, passing it would seem from north of Amarah, bypassing the marshland area. The Al Chathir of the Diz and Karkhah regions of Khuzistan are said to be an offshoot of the Al Kathir branch of the Dhafir of the area of Nasiriyyah, the Bani Lam are represented on the Persian side by the Khazraj (Khazray) and Chinanah divisions and other smaller groups also claim such links, though I have had no opportunity to see if there is any resemblance between their dialects.

Fourthly, the town of Zubair, in the desert to the southwest of Basra away from the river network, constitutes the most northward urban extension of Najdi speech linked to neighbouring Kuwait and forming an important traditional port of call for the Bedouin of the high desert.

The sea border between Iran and the Arabian peninsula is equally a zone of interaction between Arab and Persian populations and language, and here the picture is just as involved. Arabic-speaking tribal populations of the Sunni persuasion are said to live along the coastline and may also nomadize in the Barr Faris.[11] Here, however, one must be careful about confusing the ethnic label "Arab" with the designation "Arabic speaking". In parts of Fars, as also in Afghanistan, there are rural tribal populations known as Arabs, not all of whom speak Arabic, though in fact even in Afghanistan and central Asia some of these still do.[12] Another case is that of the Hwilah. In the 16th century, in the time of the prosperous Zand dynasty, and probably from even earlier times, many Arab families from the east coast of Arabia travelled to the Persian side of the Gulf and settled there, becoming considerably Persianized in the process, and would also seem to have intermarried with the Persian population. At a later date, after the eclipse of the Zand, many of these came back to the Arabian side of the Gulf. However, their Persian connection is still recognized and some families still bear names that signal an earlier Persian location. Many such families are found in the Gulf states and al-Hasa.[13] As a group they are known as the Hwilah (sing. Holi) and are distinguished both from Arab populations who do not have such a connection and from purely Persian elements of long standing, living on the Arab side of the Gulf, known as Ajam. The designation Ajam incidentally in modern parlance in the Gulf states distinguishes these latter from Irani, who are more recent post-oil era Iranian immigrants.

Although not an easy statement to substantiate, it seems that in many ways communications between the Persian coast of the Gulf and the Arab side are easier than between the Persian coast and the interior of Iran. The sea passage is reasonably easy, there being no strong tides and very few marine hazards, while the trip inland from the Gulf is arduous and the area was historically often dominated by nomadic tribes. The Persian coast is itself an inhospitable one, where good water is hard to find, the climate is unpleasant and illness and disease are rife, resulting in a tendency for the central government to neglect the area historically. Hence it has often come under Arab influence and the Persian government was quite content to allow the British to exercise considerable control in the Gulf from Bushire in the 19th century. In the 18th and early 19th centuries the Arab maritime leader Rhama bin Jabir had his main centre of influence on the Persian side at Bushire and Lengeh, and the Qawasim of Trucial Oman controlled the southern Persian coast for long periods. Trade between these two sides of the Gulf has always been substantial, lately carried on by small motorized dhow and even during the Iran–Iraq war this continued.

Conclusion

The above illustrates the quite widespread and multifarious links between "Arabia" and "Persia" in the most general sense along linguistic and ethnic lines in the region. The influences by no means go all one way. Modern Persian is full of Arabic loan words of great antiquity in the religious, literary and administrative/legal fields, while the modern spoken dialects of Arabic in Iraq, the Gulf states and even central Arabia show the influence of Persian in the realm of material culture.

Notes

1. One other good example of this is Missouri and lower Mississippi, which form the core of the Siouan linguistic stock.
2. B. Ingham, "Regional and social factors in the dialect geography of southern Iraq and Khuzistan", *Bulletin of SOAS* **39** (1976), 62–82; B. Ingham, *Northeast Arabian dialects* (London: Kegan Paul International, 1982).
3. A. H. Layard, "Description of the province of Khuzistan", *Journal of the Royal Geographical Society* **16** (1846), 29, 45.
4. This accretion of foreign elements into Arab tribes is not unknown even in more recent times. In the first half of the 19th century, at the time of the first Turkish domination of eastern Arabia after a battle fought between the Turks and Arab forces, a number of children who had been with a defeated Turkish force were captured by the Dhafir tribe. It is remembered only that these were blond and Christian, and must probably have been Armenian or Circassian. They were adopted into the tribe and eventually given Dhafiri brides. Their descendants, numbering around 40 families, are known as the Ansar (Christians), although they are now Muslims. They are still recognizably foreign looking because of their ruddy complexion but are now counted as Dhafiris and Saudi citizens. See B. Ingham, *Bedouin of northern Arabia: traditions of the Al Dhafir*, 38 (London: Kegan Paul International, 1986).
5. Layard, op. cit., 29.
6. Baron C. A. de Bode, *Travels in Luristan and Arabistan*, 188–9 (London: J. Hadden, 1845).
7. J. H. Stocqueler, *Fifteen months pilgrimage through untrodden tracts of Khuzistan and Persia*, 80 (London: Saunders & Otley, 1832).
8. A. Rush, *Al Sabah*, 186 (London: Ithaca Press, 1987).

9. W. K. Loftus, *Travels and researches in Chaldaea and Susiana*, 430 (London: James Nisbet, 1857).
10. Layard, op. cit., 35.
11. This information I have by report only from informants in Qatar, who prior to the Iran–Iraq war used to go often on hunting trips in that area and often met these people, some of whom claimed a connection with the Bani Tamim tribe.
12. T. J. Barfield, *The central Asian Arabs of Afghanistan* (Austin: University of Texas Press, 1981); W. Fischer, "Die Sprache der arabische Sprachinsel in Uzbekistan", *Der Islam* **36** (1961), 232–63; B. Ingham, "The effect of language contact on the Arabic dialect of Afghanistan", Paper presented at Congreso Internacional Interferencias Linguisticas Arabo-Romances y Paraleleos Extra-Ibericos, Madrid 1990.
13. J. G. Lorimer, *Gazetteer of the Persian Gulf, Oman and central Arabia*, vol. 8,ii, 754 (Calcutta: Superintendent Government Printing Press, 1908).

CHAPTER NINE

Iran's maritime boundaries in the Persian Gulf
The case of Abu Musa island

PIROUZ MOJTAHED-ZADEH

Introduction

Most of Iran's maritime boundaries in the Persian Gulf and the Strait of Hormuz have already been determined. The continental shelf boundaries with Saudi Arabia were delimited in 1968, with Qatar in 1970, with Bahrain in 1972 and with Oman in 1975. There are two areas where delimitation of the continental shelf has yet to be finalized. First, the maritime boundary with Kuwait at the head of the Persian Gulf is covered by a draft agreement between Iran and Kuwait but is not in force because of continuing territorial and boundary disputes between Kuwait and Iraq on the one hand and the uncertainty of the line of the extension of the Shatt al-Arab boundary into the Gulf on the other. Secondly, the Iranian continental shelf boundary with the United Arab Emirates is beset by difficulties. Iran delimited its boundary with Dubai in 1972 but official ratification of this agreement is prevented by uncertainties arising from the *de facto* joint sovereignty of Iran and Sharjah over Abu Musa. A draft agreement also exists between Iran and the emirate of Abu Dhabi but is also rendered inoperative by the Abu Musa dispute.

In order to understand the extent of the difficulties impeding a boundary settlement between Iran and its Gulf neighbours in the UAE, it is necessary to examine the status of Abu Musa island and its role in the history of and the territorial claims made by the UAE as it emerged as a nation-state.

The evolution of states and boundaries: Iran and the UAE

The Achaemenians consolidated their empire in the late 6th century BC. Their empire included most of the civilized world of the period, stretching from India in the east to Egypt and Libya in the west. When the Sassanians (AD 224–685) assumed power in Iran, rivalry with the Roman empire gave a fluctuating but definable western frontier for Iran in the Mesopotamian area controlled by the Iranian vassal kingdom of Hirah.[1]

Raids on Iranian possessions in the Persian Gulf began in the early Christian era and, by the time the Sassanians had consolidated their power, raids increased in frequency. Shahpur I undertook reprisal naval attacks in the Persian Gulf area but Arab incursions persisted until Shahpur II put an end to the problem. Sir Arnold Wilson, quoting early Islamic historians and geographers noted:

> The reign of Shahpur II (309–37 AD) was marked by frequent raids upon the Persian coasts by Arabs of Hajar, which then included Hasa, Qatif and Bahrain. Almost for the first time since the expedition of Sennacherib, we read of a naval expedition against these raiders in the Persian Gulf commanded by the king himself, which was completely successful.[2]

From the 4th century AD the coasts of the Lower Gulf from what is now Kuwait to the Musandam peninsula formed the southern flanks of the Persian empire.

The first Iranian dynasty in the post-Islamic era to revive this dominion was the Buyids. The Buyid rulers Ahmad Muzz Ad-Doleh (H 334–56) and his powerful nephew Azad Ad-Doleh (H 356–67) added Mesopotamia to their dominions and restored Iranian control over the southern Gulf. Their control in the region was maintained throughout the periods of the Seljuqs, Ghaznavids, Mongols, Atabakis and into the Safavid empire (AD 1051–1722). Nadir Shah Afshar (1736–47) restored stability after the fall of the Safavids and imposed peace on the southern coasts of the Persian Gulf. Thus the Iranian side claims a long history of control and management of the waters and islands of the Persian Gulf.

The emergence of the emirates

The tribes of the Musandam peninsula and the coastal areas of the lower Gulf, who had been living peacefully under Iranian rule,[3] used the opportunity provided by the assassination of Nadir Shah in 1747 to resume their attacks on adjacent areas. This disturbed situation continued until Karim Khan Zand established his authority in the central and southern provinces of Iran in 1757. Unlike Nadir Shah, the Khan of Zand preferred to build up friendship and co-operation with the Arabs on both shores of the Gulf as a means of gaining support for his struggle for power in Iran. His leniency towards the Arab tribes of the south helped the Qawasim (Qasimis) to gain paramountcy in the subsequent period. The Qawasim began organized intervention in maritime trade and commerce in an effective manner. Their sea power grew substantially during the 19th century.

The British established themselves as the major power in the Indian Ocean in the 19th century and imposed their control over the Persian Gulf and the Straits of Hormuz to ensure the security of their routes to India, using the pretext of eradicating piracy in the lower Gulf as their reason for intervention. British naval units, commanded by General William Grant Keir, attacked Jolfar and defeated Qasimi forces in 1819. A Treaty of Truce was signed in February 1820 by the British and the five tribal leaders of the Musandam peninsula under which these tribes came under British protection. Articles 3, 6 and 10 of this treaty provided some hints of recognition by the British of the tribal units as political entities independent of each other and of neighbouring states. Article 3, for example, allowed the tribal chiefs who signed the treaty to "carry on by land and sea a red flag, with or without letters on it".[4] This was to become the flag of the independent tribes, although their progress to recognition as territorial states was delayed for more than a century. When in 1864 the authorities controlling the independent telegraph line being set up in the area suggested that the boundaries of the Trucial states should be defined to ensure the security of the scheme, Colonel Lewis Pelly, the British Political Resident in the Persian Gulf, opposed the idea on the grounds that use of such European ideas was "inexpedient" in eastern Arabia and would result in complications.[5] A well informed and shrewd politician, Pelly knew that the issue of sovereignty in the Musandam peninsula would be better left without a territorial dimension. J. B. Kelly summarized this situation at a later date:

> The concept of territorial sovereignty in the western sense did not exist in Eastern Arabia. A ruler exercised jurisdiction over a territory by virtue of his jurisdiction over the tribes inhabiting it. They, in turn, owed loyalty to him . . . his [the tribesman's] loyalty is personal to his tribe, his Sheikh or a leader of greater consequence and not to any abstract image of state.[6]

With this background to the political geography of the Musandam peninsula in mind, it is not difficult to understand how a tribe gave loyalty to two different rulers at the same time or offered loyalty to a particular sovereign on a seasonal basis. Writing on the political status of the tribes of northern Musandam, Lorimer asserted:

> From local enquiries . . . it seemed certain that Kumzar and Khasab on the western coast, together with the villages between them, actually acknowledge the sovereignty of the Sultanate of Oman; but some doubts remain as to the status of the inhabitants of Film, Shabus and Shisah on the eastern side of the promontory, who were said to be virtually independent while at home and to become subjects of the Sheikh of Sharjah in the date season.[7]

The Qasimis of what was later to become Sharjah, like other tribes of the Musandam peninsula, continued their traditionally vague connection with the rulers of Muscat in the first half of the 19th century, whereas the rulers of Muscat themselves had some similar vague arrangement with the Iranians.

While the Sultan of Muscat administered territories around Bandar Abbas and Chah Bahar on the southern coast of Iran in the form of a lease arrangement with the Iranian government,[8] their forces also attacked and occupied places in the lower Gulf, including Bahrain on behalf of the Iranian government.

The Qasimi shaikhs in 1864 signed a separate treaty with the British, whereby they fell under British protection and their foreign relations were restricted to those with the British. This treaty underscored Sharjah's political status as an emirate independent of all others in the region. The name Sharjah came into general use at this time. The tacit acceptance of some aspects of sovereignty attaching to Sharjah did not extend to the acceptance of Qasimi territorial claims. It was not until 1866, when Shaikh Sultan Bin Saqar (1803–66) was on his deathbed, that he appointed his sons and brothers as his representatives in the towns of Ras al-Khaimah, Dibah, Kalbah and Khor Fakkan, urging them to obey his elder son Shaikh Saqar in the event of his death.[9]

Ras al-Khaimah was separated from Sharjah a year later in 1867 but was reincorporated into Sharjah in 1900. Twenty-one years later, Ras al-Khaimah was again separated from Sharjah and remained a distinct entity thereafter. Fujairah claimed separate status from Sharjah in 1901 but continued to pay tribute until 1952, when its distinct identity was finally recognized by the British. The eastern district of Kalbah claimed independence from Sharjah but was ultimately incorporated within Sharjah in 1951. Political squabbles between the emirates encouraged the British to introduce European concepts of sovereignty and national boundaries into the region.

In 1954, J. F. Walker, a British arbitrator, was assigned to carry out a survey of territorial divisions and boundary delimitation enquiries. Rulers of the seven emirates undertook to abide by his findings and awards. In a conversation with this writer in 1991, Julian Walker confirmed that he began his work in 1955 and studied 36 areas. He was able to recommend final awards in 20 cases and arranged limited formal agreements in another seven cases. As a result of Julian Walker's survey, the British Political Agent in the Emirates, J. P. Tripp, addressed letters in 1956, 1957 and 1958 to the rulers of the emirates informing them of his awards of their territorial limits and boundary arrangements. The end result of this activity by the British was a complicated patchwork of separate emirates with their dependencies and enclaves, including at least four neutral zones (Fig. 9.1).

The conversion of the Musandam peninsula from traditional to westernized systems of sovereignty and territoriality was described by John Wilkinson in the following way:

> This ludicrous partitioning of territory is of relative recent origins
> and stems in large measure from the imposing of European notions of

104

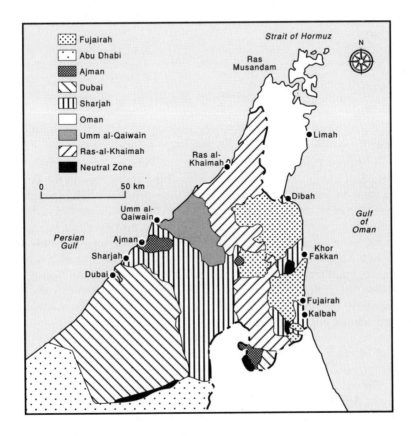

Figure 9.1 States and boundaries in the Musandam peninsula.

territorialism on a society to which they were foreign. The ad hoc process by which this happened started a century and a half ago when Britain initiated a series of treaties with the Sultan of Muscat and the coastal sheikhs of northern Oman, with the purpose of limiting their maritime activities and foreign relationships. Subsequently, as Britain sought to develop an exclusive influence in the Gulf and, later still, to favour the claims of particular companies to act as concessionaires for oil exploration, she was forced first into defending her protégé coastal rulers from attack from the hinterland and then of proclaiming their authority over the population and resources of "Greater Oman", by dividing it into a number of territories subject to them. This is not to imply that the embryonic states she helped create were entirely artificial. Rather it is to imply that from the start the terms of reference by which they came into existence more or less disregarded important aspects of traditional organisation within the region, and became increasingly irrelevant in the changing circumstances of the twentieth century.[10]

Iran's strategic position in the Strait of Hormuz

The announcement by the British government in 1968 of its decision to abandon its maintenance of the *Pax Britannica* from the area east of Suez made the future maintenance of peace in the Persian Gulf the main preoccupation of foreign and regional policies of the states around the Gulf.

Because the Persian Gulf is connected to the open seas solely through the narrow Strait of Hormuz, security threats from the outside world via the sea route cannot be prevented without an effective control over this strait. Iran sees itself better placed than any other country of the region for the protection of the Strait of Hormuz. From the Iranian point of view, this is largely because, apart from being the strongest military power of the region, and controlling the entire northern coast of the Persian Gulf, Iran can also protect the straits and its approaches from its military positions on strategically situated islands near Hormuz.

Iran is in possession of a number of islands situated at the entrance of the Strait of Hormuz, of which six islands of the so-called "curved line" are of greatest significance. These are the islands of Hormuz, Hengam, Qeshm, Larak, Greater Tunb and Abu Musa. Iran's strategy has been to utilize these islands as defensive posts by maintaining its armed forces there.

An imaginary line (Fig. 9.2) drawn alongside these islands, which are situated within a relatively short distance from one another, makes it easy to appreciate how effectively the shipping lanes of the Strait of Hormuz can be covered by the Iranian fire power stationed on these islands. The islands of Hormuz, Hengam, Qeshm and Larak have been the subject of many studies.[11] This chapter will thus concentrate solely on a brief discussion of the political geography and history of the islands of Tunb and Abu Musa.

Greater Tunb[12]

Lying 31 km southwest of Qeshm, the island of Tunb is situated on the north of the Gulf's median line, 50 km from the Iranian port of Bandar Lengeh and more than 70 km from the Emirate of Ras al-Khaimah. The word "tunb" in the Tangestani (South Persian) dialect means hill. Since Tunb is located relatively far from the entrance of the Persian Gulf, its individual strategic value is not significant; rather it is valuable as part of the general Iranian defence line at the entrance to the Strait of Hormuz (Fig. 9.3).

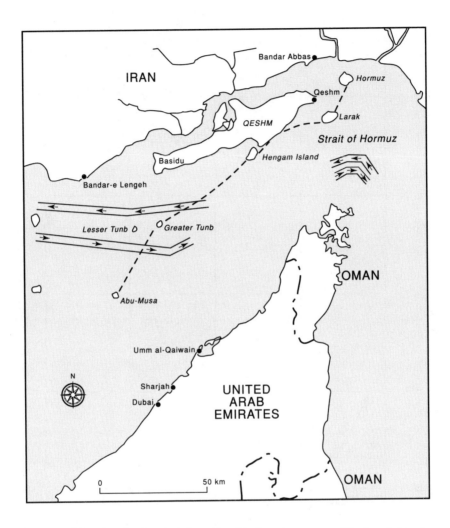

Figure 9.2 Map showing Iran's defence line (the imaginary curved line) and shipping lanes in the Persian Gulf and the Straits of Hormuz.

Lesser Tunb[13]

Lesser Tunb, an uninhabited rock only 35 m high, lies a few kilometres southwest of Greater Tunb. It has significance as a connecting point secondary to Greater Tunb in the Iranian defence ring of islands at the entrance of the Gulf.

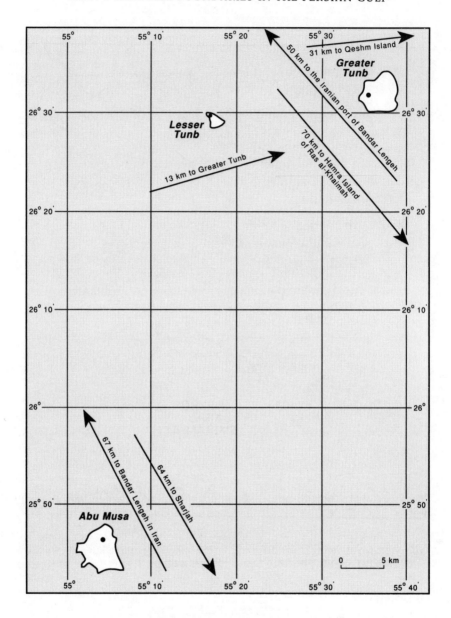

Figure 9.3 The islands of Abu Musa, Greater and Lesser Tunb.

Island of Abu Musa

This is the most westerly of the six islands, the last point of the Iranian strategic defence line. It lies between longitude 55°01'E–55°04'E and latitude 25°51'N–25°54'N. It is situated at 50 km east of Sirri island, 67 km south of Bandar Lengeh and about 64 km from the port of Sharjah (Fig. 9.3).

Abu Musa is larger than the two Tunbs, almost rectangular in shape and about 5 km across diagonally. This island is relatively low-lying, consisting of sandy plains, especially to the south and centre. It is grazed by domestic animals and gazelle. The surface of the island is uneven, with hills rising towards the north that culminate in Mount Halva, a volcanic feature some 110 m high. There is fresh water from a number of wells and date palm plantations are a familiar sight. Abu Musa is particularly well known for its deposits of red iron oxide. The first concession for its exploitation was given to a native of Bandar Lengeh by the Qasimi Shaikh of Lengeh for an annual royalty of £250. This concession was later given to Haj Moin Bushehri, a famous Iranian industrialist of the turn of the 20th century, after the Qasimi autonomy of Bandar Lengeh was abolished in 1887. Lorimer estimated the number of Iranians working these mines at the time as 100 and the average amount of oxide removed annually as 40,000 bags.[14]

Concessions for exploitation of the ore were then given to the German company Wönckhaus (1912) and then to the British company Golden Valley Colour Ltd and a Japanese company. All these concessions were granted by the Shaikh of Sharjah and endorsed by Iran following the Iran–Sharjah Memorandum of Understanding of November 1971.

Abu Musa's oil is produced from the nearby Mubarak field and is the best-quality oil produced in the Persian Gulf. It is produced from three wells by Buttes Oil and Gas Company. The concession for this was granted by Sharjah and endorsed by Iran in December 1971 on the understanding that all profits from the exploitation would be divided equally between Iran and Sharjah.

Following the November 1971 Iran–Sharjah Memorandum of Understanding and the partial restoration of Iran's sovereignty rights to the island, Iran's 12 nautical mile territorial water limit was applied to Abu Musa. Application of this territorial water limit overlapped that of the emirate of Umm al-Qaiwain, where an exploration concession had been given to the Occidental Oil Company in 1969. A solution was found to the problem by Iran based on a median line where the two territorial limits overlapped.

Abu Musa's permanent population of 600 is made up of Iranians of Lengeh origin and Arabs of Sharjah origin from the Sudan tribe of the village of Khan in Sharjah. The November 1971 memorandum places the inhabitants of Abu Musa under Sharjah's sovereignty and the strategic parts of the island under Iran's sovereignty.

Historical background

The decline of Safavid power in the early 18th century created great disturbance throughout Iran. The confused state of affairs around Bandar Abbas and Hormuz in the 1720s was used by the Qasimi Shaikh of Musandam to found a port of his own at Basa'idu on Qeshm island. Nadir Shah's rise to power in 1736 secured stability in Iran and restored Iran's sovereignty in and around the Persian Gulf.

Iran's control of its ports and islands in the Persian Gulf was put in jeopardy once again in the chaos following Nadir Shah's assassination in June 1747, when a number of local chiefs used the opportunity to increase their autonomy. One such figure was the Iranian admiral Mulla Ali Shah, who managed to establish himself as the governor of Hormuz. He refused to pay tribute to the Iranian central government as early as 1747 and sought alliance, by marriage, with the powerful Qawasim shaikhs of Jolfar (now Ras al-Khaimah) on the Musandam coast. In 1751 the Qasimi shaikh sent a fleet to the northern shores of the Strait of Hormuz, seemingly to pay a courtesy call on Mulla Ali upon the marriage of his daughter, but in reality to expand his influence on the Iranian shores of the northern Gulf. When in 1759 robbers attacked the British Political Agent's residence in Bandar Abbas, the East India Company sought redress from Karim Khan Zand. Shaikh Nasir Khan, Governor of Lar, was assigned by the Iranian court to curb the upstart activities at Bandar Abbas and Hormuz. War inevitably broke out between his forces and those of Mulla Ali Shah. An army of 1,000 Arabs, commanded personally by the Qawasim Shaikh of Jolfar, landed at Bandar Abbas in support of Mulla Ali. As the war dragged on, a branch of the Qawasim managed to establish itself at Lengeh. The islands of Kish, Tunb, Abu Musa and Sirri had always been dependencies of the governorship of Lengeh; therefore the Qasimi authorities at Lengeh, like all those before and after them, included these islands as well as the coastal ports of Laft and Kang.

As time went by, the Qasimis of Lengeh maintained good relations with their cousins in Jolfar, while at the same time they succeeded in becoming governors of Lengeh, administering affairs of the province on behalf of the central government of Iran.

Karim Khan Zand (1757–99) was tolerant towards the autonomous Arab tribes on the Iranian coast. He actually sought assistance from them in his struggle for power. Karim Khan's leaning towards the Arab tribes meanwhile helped the Qawasim of both shores to achieve prominence in late 18th century and early 19th century.

The Qasimis of the Musandam coasts expanded their piratical activities at sea in the early years of the 19th century and threatened merchant ships of all nations, including commercial vessels belonging to British India. The increase in piracy gave British India the opportunity to impose peace in the

Persian Gulf by destroying the bases from which the pirates operated. Jolfar was captured in 1819 and a treaty of peace was signed in February 1820 between General Sir William Grant Keir, commander of the British expeditionary force, and rulers of five shaikhdoms of Musandam at the time, including the Qasimi Shaikh of Sharjah.

This General Treaty of Truce, together with a series of bilateral treaties signed thereafter, put these emirates under the protection of Britain, while the Qawasim of Lengeh remained subjects of Iran. Having established its control over the Musandam coasts, Britain decided to send an expeditionary force to Lengeh to subjugate the Qawasim of the Iranian coast. The Iranian authorities opposed this action on the grounds that the Qasimi shaikhs of Lengeh were Iranian subjects:

> To prevent any misunderstanding on the part of the Persian Government of the object of the British expedition – particularly operations against the Sheikhs of Lengeh and Charak – a special emissary, Dr. Dukes was dispatched in advance with reassuring letters from the governor of Bombay for the governor general of Fars and the Persian governor of Bushire. Another letter was sent to the British chargé d'affaires in Tehran, to enable him to inform the Shah. The Shah, however, was not appeased and the Prince of Shiraz wrote to Keir requesting him to refrain from interference at any of his ports, especially Lengeh. Keir therefore thought it [inadvisable] to land troops on the Persian soil.[15]

This development left the British in no doubt that Lengeh and its dependencies were integral parts of Iran. This fact was demonstrated particularly in the form of a map produced in 1835 by the acting British Political Resident in the Persian Gulf, Captain S. Hennell. In order to prevent conflicts among the Arab tribes of the southern coasts of the Persian Gulf during the pearl-fishing period of that year, Captain Hennell suggested a maritime truce, which was signed on 21 August 1835. He drew a line on the map of the Persian Gulf separating possessions of the Arab tribes from those of Iran. His map specified the ports of Lengeh, Laft, Kang and Charak as well as the islands of Qeshm, Tunbs and Abu Musa as possessions of Iran, thus recognizing Iran's sovereignty over these islands. A similar map was produced at a later date by Major Morrison, who introduced a new line of territorial specification in the regions that started from Ras az-Zur near Kuwait to Sir Bu Na'ir island of Sharjah, then continuing to Ash-Shams near Ras Musandam. This line, too, showed the three islands of the Tunbs and Abu Musa and the Qasimi governorate of Lengeh within Iran's jurisdiction. The Qasimis of Lengeh, in the meantime, demonstrated their loyalty to the Iranian government and assisted Iranian expeditions on various occasions against rebellious Arab tribes of the region. Another map produced by the British Admiralty in 1881 painted the islands of Tunbs and Abu Musa in the same colour as Lengeh and the rest of the Iranian mainland.

The Iranian government decided, in 1885, that the old Safavid administrative organization of the country was no longer viable in the modern world. A new administrative organization was introduced that divided the country into 27 *ayalats* or provinces, of which the 26th *ayalat* was the Province of the Ports of the Persian Gulf.[16] In 1885 Shaikh Yusuf Qasimi, who had ruled in Lengeh since 1878, was murdered by his relative, Shaikh Qadhib Bin Rashid. This event made the Iranian government decide to put an end to the Qasimi autonomy in Lengeh and its dependencies and to include the area under the direct control of the 26th *ayalat*. Tehran's first step was to increase its direct involvement in the affairs of Lengeh. This policy seems to have been adopted by the new governor-general of the 26th *ayalat*, Amin as-Sultan:

> The years 1887 and 1888 were signalised, as we have already seen, by a spasmodic attempt on the part of the Persian Government to assert themselves in the politics of the Persian Gulf. The prime mover in this undertaking seems to have been the Shah's favourite, the Amino us-Sultan, to whom the Government of the Gulf Ports has been entrusted; and indications of his ambition of reducing foreign influence were naturally soon manifested in the Persian district under his jurisdiction, as well as in foreign relations.[17]

In 1887 Shaikh Qadhib al-Qasimi was arrested, on instructions from Amin as-Sultan, for the murder of Shaikh Yusuf. He was taken in chains to Tehran where he died, thus bringing to an end the Qasimi autonomy of Lengeh, which was entrusted to a new governor appointed by Amin as-Sultan.

In 1898 Shaikh Muhammad, son of a former Qasimi governor of Lengeh (Shaikh Khalifah Bin Said), seized Lengeh and held it for about a year until he was expelled by the Iranian authorities. Shaikh Muhammad was reported to have been in the vicinity of the Trucial states trying to muster a force that could take him back to Lengeh. The Iranian government asked the British government to prevent any act of aggression from the southern side of the Gulf against Iranian territories at Lengeh or at any other part of the Iranian coasts. The British government accordingly issued warnings to the shaikhs of the Trucial states not to interfere in the affairs of Iran by assisting Shaikh Mohammad. In 1900 the Iranian governor-general of the province of Persian Gulf Ports established cordial correspondence with the Shaikh of Abu Dhabi, aiming to isolate him from the other rulers of the Trucial states, to prevent any attack on Lengeh. Shaikh Zaid Ben Khalifah of Abu Dhabi was concerned in this relationship to secure favourable Iranian consideration of claims by some of his subjects to properties in Iran. The shaikhs of Sharjah and Dubai, apparently still unhappy about the events in Lengeh, reported the matter to Khan Bahador Abdul-Latif, British Political Agent in the Persian Gulf. They argued that Shaikh Zaid's friendly correspondence with the Iranian government was a breach of the bilateral agreement of 1892 between

Britain and Abu Dhabi, Article 1 of which prevented the Shaikh from "entering any agreement or correspondence with any party other than the British Government".[18] The Ruler of Abu Dhabi was cautioned and that particular correspondence ceased.

The politically efficacious use of the British representatives in the region encouraged the Qasimi shaikhs of Sharjah to try and salvage as much territory formerly administered by their tribal cousins as possible. For example, the British had constructed a lighthouse on Greater Tunb and looking after it put the island under their closer inspection. The Qasimi shaikhs of Sharjah were given permission to hunt on the islands of Tunbs and Abu Musa by the British Political Agent. The British recognized in 1903 that the islands of Tunbs and Abu Musa belonged to the Shaikh of Sharjah. Iran was at that time on the verge of civil war. The authority of the central government had declined to an all-time low and a popular uprising eventually resulted in the 1906 Constitutional Revolution, which preoccupied Tehran with domestic affairs. The Qasimi shaikh of Sharjah therefore hoisted his flag on those islands without opposition of consequence from the Iranians.

In April 1904 Iran's Director of Customs, Mr Damberian, visited Abu Musa and was surprised to see Sharjah's flag flying. He replaced it with the Iranian flag and installed Iranian customs guards, apparently with the sanction of the Iranian foreign minister. The Qasimi shaikh was disturbed, and the British legation in Tehran made representations with threats on behalf of Sharjah. The embattled and weakened government in Tehran ordered the withdrawal of the guards and the lowering of the flag. Within a few days Sharjah's flag was hoisted again and the British "regarded the two islands as belonging to the states of Sharjah and Ras al-Khaimah".[19] The transfer of the islands to the Qasimis of Musandam was done on the basis that the islands of Tunbs and Abu Musa "had formerly been ruled by the hereditary Arab governors of Lengeh in their capacity as Qasimi shaikhs rather than as Persian officials".[20] Following the Constitutional Revolution, Iran found it too late and itself too weak to bring about a reversal of the British decision and remained unhappy about the whole affair, especially as illegal trade through these islands to the Iranian mainland increased. The Iranian customs office made representations to the government in July 1927, demanding action against the illegal trade by establishing guards on the three islands.[21] A fleet of the newly founded Iranian navy was sent in 1928 to recover Abu Musa and the two Tunbs and to put an end to the problems there. This action resulted in the start of a series of Anglo–Iranian negotiations over these islands that lasted for many years.

The return of the two Tunbs to Iran in 1934

In 1934 the Governor of Bandar Abbas and other Iranian officials visited Greater Tunb in a dhow. This visit was the result of a secret arrangement with the Shaikh of Ras al-Khaimah by the Iranians according to which the shaikh lowered his flag on Greater Tunb and the Iranian flag was hoisted in its place. Subsequently a Trucial coast dhow was seized by an Iranian warship in Tunb's territorial waters and on four occasions that year an Iranian warship visited the island, twice to land Iranians there. These activities attracted the attention of the British, who vigorously protested against what was going on there and orally informed the Iranian government that it would as a last resort protect the interests of the Trucial shaikhs by force.[22] Reporting these events to his government, the British minister at Tehran stated:

> Some mysterious happenings took place at [Tunb] in the early part of the year following the action of the Sheikh of Ras al-Khaimah at the end of 1934 in having his flagstaff removed. There being grounds for suspicion that the Sheikh had been intriguing with the Iranians the senior naval officer landed a small guard and, though this was later withdrawn, for some weeks a sloop visited the island at frequent intervals.[23]

However, the British intervened at the end of this episode and averted further complication by promising that no flag would be hoisted on the islands until the issue was settled peacefully.[24]

A consideration of Iran's historical claims to the islands

The two Tunbs and Abu Musa were not the only islands of the northern Gulf used in the 19th and first half of the 20th centuries by the British, either directly or through assumed sovereignty of the Trucial emirates. Qeshm, Hengam and Sirri islands were also objects of contention between Iran and Britain.

Qeshm was the first Iranian island of the Persian Gulf to be used by the British. Having crushed the power of Arab pirates in the southern Gulf in 1819, British General Grant Keir transferred his forces, originally 1,200 strong, to Qeshm island. This move was strongly protested about by the Iranians, who called upon the British to evacuate the island. This appeal was ignored, and in 1923 the British established a naval supply depot at Basidu on the northwestern tip of the island.[25] When the British decided to establish the Indo–European telegraph line, which passed through the coasts and islands of the Persian Gulf, they negotiated with the Iranian authorities for a cable station on Hengam in 1868. For reasons of their own they closed the station in 1880 but 24 years later reoccupied the old site, removed the Iranian flag and hoisted the Union Jack in its place.[26] Qeshm island was recovered by the Iranians at a later date.

The history of Sirri island is similar to that of the two Tunbs and Abu Musa. Like the other three islands, Sirri was assumed by the British in 1887 to be the territory of the emirate of Sharjah.

A War Office map, presented by the British Minister [at Tehran] to the Shah in 1888, showed all the islands [the two Tunbs, Abu Musa and Sirri] in Persian colours: the Persian case was further strengthened with the publication in 1892 of Curzon's two-volume *Persia and the Persian Question* in which the map, prepared by the Royal Geographical Society under Curzon's own supervision, also showed the islands as Persian territory.[27]

The Iranians, however, occupied Sirri island in 1887, but their occupation of that island was removed by the British at a later date. The Iranians also tried to establish customs posts and hoist a flag on the Greater Tunb and Abu Musa in 1904, but abandoned the attempt in the face of a strong British protest.[28]

It was rumoured in 1905 that Iran had ceded, sold or leased Qeshm island to the Russians,[29] but the rumour proved to be unfounded. Early in January 1906 the Darya Begi Amir Tuman, Governor of Persian Gulf Ports and Islands, and Haj Moin Bushehri directed the headman of Qeshm island to instruct the inhabitants of Hengam island to pay the customs authorities the revenue or any other taxes demanded by the latter.[30] This move was discontinued as a result of British protest.

Iran's claim of sovereignty regarding Tunbs, Abu Musa and Sirri,which was first asserted in 1887 in response to a claim to the contrary made by the British, was reasserted in 1904 after the discovery by the Iranians of a Sharjah flag on these islands and resumed in 1923, 1926 and 1927. In 1929 the British Foreign Office prepared a draft article for inclusion in a proposed treaty with Iran that would have provided for the recognition of the sovereignty of the Qasimi shaikhs of Musandam coasts over the islands of Tunb and Abu Musa in return for recognition of Iranian sovereignty of the island of Sirri. The Anglo–Persian Oil Company crisis of 1932 intervened and the draft of the intended treaty was abandoned in 1934.[31] In 1933 an Iranian warship visited the island of Greater Tunb and landed a party which inspected the lighthouse there. This exercise was repeated in 1934 when the Shaikh of Ras al-Khaimah returned the two Tunbs to Iran. This development angered the British. Sir R. Hoare, British diplomat at Tehran, held a conference with the Iranian prime minister over the issue during which he notified the Iranian prime minister that:

Tunb and Abu Musa were on precisely the same footing as Sirri Island so that when HMS *Ormonde* visited the Gulf for surveying purposes Her Majesty's Government requested the Iranian Government to notify their officials on Sirri Island that the vessel would also pay a visit there. A sentence was added to that communication that this did not imply a recognition of Iran's *de jure* title to the island. It was thought that the Iranians might refer the case to the Council of the League of Nations but they did not.[32]

The reason for the British apprehension that the Iranians might have wanted to refer the case to the League of Nations was that the Iranians had in 1929 offered to refer the case to international arbitration but the British had turned the offer down. Reporting his talks with Teimurtash, Riza Shah's famous Minister of Imperial Court, Sir Robert Clive, British Minister Plenipotentiary at Tehran, wrote in January 1939 to Sir Austin Chamberlain, stating:

> Then we talked about the islands of Tunb and Abu Musa and I asked the Court Minister what benefit did the Government of Iran seem to have in taking these islands other than claiming that smugglers in the Persian Gulf are using them as their base for storing goods and smuggling them into Iran. Teimurtash answered that the Government of Iran did not see this matter in the same way as we do, but their main point is that these islands are the indivisible parts of Iran and are occupied by others by force. I answered Teimurtash in accordance with the guideline that you had sent me. The Court Minister said in that case there is no other way but to refer the matter to an international arbitration. Replying to His Excellency I expressed hopes that the two sides could settle their differences without having to refer the case to international arbitration . . .[33]

Negotiations continued until mid-spring 1929 without much progress being made. The Conservative government of Mr Baldwin was replaced in May of that year by a Labour administration, with Arthur Henderson replacing Chamberlain as Britain's foreign secretary. Mr Henderson showed less flexibility towards the British colonial role in the Persian Gulf and brought the negotiations with the Iranian authorities on the issue of Abu Musa and the Tunbs to an abrupt end. This development did not, however, deter the Iranian side from seeking to recover the islands.

At the end of 1948 the Iranians expressed a wish to place administrative offices on Tunb and Abu Musa. In 1949 there were rumours first that the Iranians were preparing to refer the case to the United Nations and later that they intended to occupy the islands by force. The Iranian government subsequently received a note from the British embassy in Tehran expressing the British government's "clear attitude" in that respect.[34] The Iranians, in return, erected a flagstaff on Lesser Tunb in August of that year, which was promptly removed by the Royal Navy.

In 1953, during Mussadiq's second term of premiership, there were reports in the Iranian press that an Iranian commission was to be sent to Abu Musa. An Iranian warship landed a party on that island and made enquiries of the inhabitants. Once again the British notified the Iranian authorities that Abu Musa was subject to the Shaikh of Sharjah. Early in 1953 reports were received by the British that the Iranians were contemplating the dispatch of troops to occupy the two Tunb islands, Abu Musa and Sirri and reconnaissance flights were carried out over these islands by the Royal Air Force.[35]

On 18 May 1961, during the premiership of Dr Ali Amini, an Iranian helicopter landed on Greater Tunb. As this move was not protested against by the British authorities, an Iranian launch landed on the island on 9 August 1961. On the first occasion, a helicopter hired by the Iranians from a British company brought in an Iranian and two American subjects, who photographed the lighthouse and adjacent buildings. They talked to the lighthouse keeper but entered no building and accepted no hospitality.[36] On the second occasion, according to a report by British naval officers, the Iranian launch approached from the east, landed a party on the eastern coast of the island but soon withdrew and went to the south where a party was landed at a village. Two of the visitors were described by the locals as Americans, and the second landing was thought to have been connected with an oil survey.[37]

The British protested against the Iranian actions[38] and later demanded an explanation for the landings.[39] Finally, on 5 September 1961, the British embassy in Tehran handed the Iranian Ministry of Foreign Affairs a note of protest on behalf of the Shaikh of Ras al-Khaimah.[40] The Iranian government reacted on 21 September 1961 by declaring that:

> As the Embassy is aware, the Imperial Iranian Government have never accepted the claim that the island of Tunb is a part of the Sheikhdom of Ras al-Khaimah or that any other state has a right over it. As has been officially declared to the Embassy on many occasions, the Imperial Government of Iran consider the island of Tunb to be part of their own territory over which they have sovereignty. The Imperial Government's sovereignty over the island of Tunb is based on the rules and principles of International Law and they have never given up their right to it. In the above circumstances the Imperial Ministry of Foreign Affairs do not consider the Embassy's protest as contained in the note under reference to be justified.[41]

The British Foreign Office repeated its protest in the hope that "the Iranians will get tired of this sort of exchange before we do".[42] This second note of 13 January 1962[43] was replied to in the same vein by the Iranians. A year later, when Amir Assadollah Alam was premier, the Iranians occupied Sirri in spite of objections by the British and the Shaikh of Sharjah.

The seizure of the Tunbs and Abu Musa

Iran resumed its agitation for the "return of the Tunbs and Abu Musa to Iran" in early 1970. The Bahrain dispute had been settled in that year and it was widely believed that this had been done so that the British would acquiesce in an Iranian occupation of Abu Musa and the Tunbs. As early as 1968 there were Arab suspicions on this matter, and *Al-Ahram* speculated in November "if it were true that Britain had imposed an agreement regarding the Bahrain issue by giving the island of Abu Musa to Iran as the price for dropping its claims to Bahrain".[44]

There is no doubt that Iran's conciliatory attitude with regard to Bahrain was prompted by its perception of larger stakes in the Strait of Hormuz, but there is no evidence suggesting that Iran and Britain had made a deal in 1968 on the future of these islands. An examination of events following the Bahrain settlement reveals that, once the matter of Iranian claims to Bahrain had been settled, Iran made the conceding of the three Gulf islands a prerequisite of its recognition of the proposed United Arab Emirates, at that stage including both Qatar and Bahrain as well as the Trucial states. Immediately after the Bahrain settlement in May 1970, Iran publicly argued its case for recognition of its rights to the islands of Abu Musa and the two Tunbs.

The Iranians and the British were discussing the settlement of Gulf affairs as they might be after the British withdrawal from east of Suez. In his confidential diary Amir Assadollah Alam made several reference to these negotiations. In his diary for Monday 18 February 1969 (Iranian date 28.11.1347), Mr Alam indicated:

> British Ambassador [Sir Denis Wright] . . . told me very confidentially that the case of Tunb island is practically settled and will definitely be given to Iran, for we have told the Sheikh of Ras al-Khaimah that if you don't come to some sort of arrangement with Iran – as these islands are situated above the median line [of the Persian Gulf] Iran will lawfully, and if that was not possible, will forcibly take these islands, and the Sheikh agreed to make a deal over them. I said: What about Abu Musa? He said: this island is situated below the median line. I said: and our power is sufficient enough to put a step below the line . . . He said: [If you resort to force] your relations with the Arabs will be harmed. I said: to hell with it . . .[45]

A measure of ambivalence on the rightful ownership of the Gulf islands can be sensed in the writings of some British officials in the Persian Gulf in the late 1950s and early 1960s. D. F. Hawley, British Political Agent for the Trucial states in 1958–61, described the ownership of the Tunb islands and Abu Musa in the following way:

> *Abu Musa.* This island is in the effective control of the ruler of Sharjah, and has been occupied by the Qawasim for several generations . . .
> *Tunb and Nabiyu Tunb.* These islands have [been] regarded as belong-

ing to Ras al-Khaimah since the ruler became independent of Sharjah in 1921.[46]

By comparison, the Iranian press was putting forward a vigorous argument on Iran's "indisputable" ownership of these islands. *Kayhan International* on 30 May 1970 reported:

> The three islands have belonged to Iran since time immemorial and have always formed an integral part of the country. About eighty years ago, the British Government, for imperialistic considerations, unlawfully and temporarily separated them from Iran by preventing Iran from exercising its established sovereign rights over them.[47]

This was an iteration of the points made earlier by the Shah. In an interview during his flight to Switzerland in early February 1971, the Shah stated:

> These islands belong to the nation, and we have British Admiralty maps and other documents which prove this. We will, if necessary, regain them by force because I don't want to witness my country to be put up to auction.[48]

In a second interview with the Indian magazine *Blitz* on 24 June 1971 the Shah declared that "the islands belonged to Iran"; they had been "grabbed some eighty years earlier at a time when Iran had no central Government", and that "his father had sent gunboats to recover them, but the British assured Iran that no flag of sovereignty would be hoisted until the question was settled". The Shah than added, "I hope this happens now. Otherwise we have no alternative but to take the islands by force."[49] A further warning of the use of force in "returning" these islands came on 27 June 1971 from Amir Abbas Huvaida, the then premier, who told the people of the strategic Gulf port of Bandar Abbas that:

> Iran was by no means indifferent to the future of the Persian Gulf, because it constituted its vital access route. Iran needed these islands for [its security and prosperity], a goal for the attainment of which Iran would fight with all its might should it fail to settle this problem by peaceful means.[50]

Despite these warnings of the use of force to recover the islands, Iran continued negotiations with the British in 1971. In November, 24 hours before an Iranian landing on the Gulf islands, the authorities in Sharjah announced an agreement with Iran, according to which Iranian forces were to take possession of strategic areas of Abu Musa. The announcement included the following points:[51]

> In order to prevent bloodshed between the two Muslim and neighbourly peoples of Iran and Sharjah, the two sides have agreed on the following specifics:
>
> (1) Iranian forces will take control of the strategic areas of the northern parts of the island as specified in the map attached to the agreement.

(2) Iran will enjoy every right of sovereignty in the said parts of the island and the Iranian flag will be hoisted there.

(3) The Emirate of Sharjah will exercise her rights of sovereignty over the southern half of the island including the village of Abu Musa and her flag will be hoisted there.

(4) Iran and Sharjah agree to recognize the breadth of the island's territorial sea as 12 nautical miles (according to Iran's law of territorial waters).

(5) The Buttes Oil and Gas Company will continue with the concession previously granted by the Emirate of Sharjah for exploration in Abu Musa's oilfields of the said territorial waters. Iran will recognize this company's concession and the company will divide equally the income from the oil exploitation between Iran and Sharjah.

(6) Citizens of Iran and Sharjah will enjoy equal rights of fishing in Abu Musa's territorial waters.

(7) A financial arrangement will take effect between Iran and Sharjah.

Iran offered to pay Sharjah £1.5 million annually for a period of nine years. This was to cease should Sharjah's oil revenues reach £3 million per annum.[52] Other sources, however, implied that this financial arrangement "included a provision that one half of the oil revenues from the island and its continental shelf should be allocated under a special arrangement for the welfare of the people of Sharjah.[53]

Since Sharjah was still a British protectorate at the time and, in accordance with the terms of its special treaty of 1892 with Great Britain, it did not have the right to sign an official agreement or treaty with any foreign power except Great Britain, it is noteworthy that the above arrangement or "understanding" between the emirate and Iran cannot be considered as an official treaty or agreement. Sharjah gained its independence within the federal framework of the United Arab Emirates on 1 December 1971. An Iranian official of the Iranian Ministry of Foreign Affairs, who wished to remain anonymous, subsequently showed the author a letter addressed by Dr Abbas-Qaoli Khalatbary, then foreign minister of Iran to Sir Alec Douglas-Home, the British foreign secretary, warning that if Iran felt at any time that activities occurring in the Sharjah-controlled section of Abu Musa threatened Iran's interests, sovereignty and security in that island, the government of Iran would reserve for themselves the right to implement their full sovereignty over the whole of Abu Musa. Replying to this letter, the British Foreign Office informed Iran that the contents of the above letter were communicated to the Shaikh of Sharjah.

Abu Musa's 12 mile territorial waters overlapped those of the Emirate of Umm al-Qaiwain. In a settlement between Iran and Sharjah on the one hand and Umm al-Qaiwain on the other, it was arranged for the latter to receive a 15 per cent share of the oil revenues from the overlapping areas.

The Memorandum of Understanding agreed between Iran and Sharjah and declared on 29 November 1971 was undoubtedly a part of the Anglo–Iranian negotiations going on prior to Iran's use of force. An Iranian government spokesman later claimed that not only Sharjah but Ras al-Khaimah had been aware of the landing of Iranian forces on the three islands.[54]

The agreement with Sharjah, however, left the status of Abu Musa undefined. In an interview with an *Al-Ahram* correspondent in Sharjah on 7 December 1971, the then ruler of the Emirate of Sharjah stated that: "Sharjah did not believe that its agreement with Iran adversely affected its sovereignty over the island", and that "the agreement was temporary and was an instrument for overcoming crisis and preventing bloodshed".[55] This statement totally contradicted an earlier statement by the Iranian premier to the Iranian *Majlis*. Premier Huvaida stated on 30 November 1971:

> The Iranian flag was unfurled on Mount Halva, the highest peak on the island of Abu Musa. I deem it necessary to declare on this occasion that the Government of H.I.M. has in no conceivable way relinquished or will relinquish its sovereign rights and incontestable jurisdiction over the whole island of Abu Musa, and hence, the presence of local agents [i.e. Sharjah officials] in a segment of the island of Abu Musa should in no way be viewed or interpreted as contradictory to this declared policy.[56]

Arab reaction to the Iranian statement was mixed. Radical Arab states adopted vociferous policies both domestically and in the United Nations, while the moderates preferred prudence. The Arab League was urged by the radicals to lodge a collective Arab complaint with the United Nations Security Council, signed by all 21 member states of the time. The proposal was opposed by the majority of the member states. Instead, they agreed to condemn Iran's action individually by issuing statements in their own capitals. All Arab states issued this statement of condemnation except Jordan, while the leaders of Egypt, Morocco, Saudi Arabia, Oman and Bahrain apologized privately to the Iranian leadership for having issued such statements.

The radical Arab states – Algeria, Iraq, Libya and former South Yemen – took their complaint to the UN Security Council, which met on 9 December 1971 to examine the case. Representatives of these four countries were joined by representatives of Kuwait and the United Arab Emirates, the latter becoming a member of the United Nations on the same day.[57]

Talib al-Shibib, representing Iraq, alleged in his account of the event that "Iran had claimed the whole Gulf, but 'such ludicrous blanket claims' had been reduced to claims on Bahrain and later the Tunbs and Abu Musa".[58] He asserted that his government had received a cable from the Shaikh of Ras al-Khaimah claiming that the two Tunbs had belonged to Ras al-Khaimah since ancient times.[59] On the other hand, the UAE representative made a very mild and conciliatory statement.[60] Abdullah Yaqub Bishara, representing Kuwait, claimed that the islands of Greater Tunb and Lesser Tunb had belonged to Ras al-Khaimah "for centuries".[61] A similar statement was made by the UAE foreign minister at the United Nations General Assembly on 30 September 1992, where it was also alleged that the islands of Tunbs and Abu Musa had belonged to the emirates "since the beginning of history".[62] It is worth observing, however, that the Emirate of Sharjah was created in 1856, the Emirate of Ras al-Khaimah in 1921 and the United Arab Emirates in 1971.

In his statement to the UN Security Council meeting of 9 December 1971, Abdellatif Rahal of Algeria presented a more rational historical account of this case by saying: "There had been conflicting claims to those islands over the years, but it was undeniable that during the whole period of British control the islands had been part of the territory that had become the United Arab Emirates."[63] This statement, albeit more rational than those made by representatives of Kuwait, Iraq and Libya, was not in complete accord with the facts of history: British control of the lower Gulf territories began in 1820, while Abu Musa and the two Tunbs were seized from Iran and given to the Qasimi tribal entity of Sharjah by the British in 1903.

For his part, Amir Khosrow Afshar, representing Iran in the hearing, made a relatively short statement rejecting the charges against Iran as baseless, and said that the question was essentially an internal matter for his country. However, he did deal with some of the points raised:

The area concerned is the Persian Gulf, not the Arabian Gulf, a term used by certain states to distort historical reality and to give the area an Arab character. The riparian states of the Persian Gulf should work together without outside interference. Iran has no territorial ambition . . . trying to settle disputes peacefully, as shown by its actions in the case of Bahrain, for which she had been praised here . . . Iraq had created a tense situation in the area in 1961 by its hostile acts against Kuwait and had carried on a provocative campaign . . . Iraq had laid claim to Kuwait and brought the matter to the United Nations. In this case, too, Iraq is taking up the Council's time for baseless claims . . . The islands [in question] are Iranian territory. Iran's title to them is long standing, and they are shown in maps hundreds of years old as Iranian. The islands are part of a group forming a virtual archipelago that has always been Iranian. One of the islands is only 17 miles offshore; another is 22 miles offshore. The nearest Arab republic, for instance is much further and Libyan Arab Republic, for instance, is thousands of miles away . . . I mention the Libyan Arab Republic because it is reported to have threatened to send troops to the area. Iraq has also said it might send troops . . . Iran would not allow its sovereignty, or a single inch of its territory to be violated.[64]

Finally, Abdulrahman Abby Farah, representative of Somalia, a member of the Arab League, proposed that the Council should adjourn consideration of the complaint to allow third-party efforts at mediation to take place. The Council agreed without objection to that course and thus the case was let to rest.

Another part of Mr Afshar's[65] statement in the UN Security Council was reported in the *Iran Almanac* of 1972, which asserts:

> For more than a century, beginning in 1870 British maps marked the Tunb islands as being Persian. In addition, a highly authoritative Encyclopaedia published as recently as 1967 to cover the events of the last fifty years, by another major power, identified the Tunbs as Iranian territory. It is important to remember that both the British map and the Encyclopaedia were published at the time of British control over the islands. The maps show the islands as having the same colour as the mainland and in addition they are expressly marked as being Iranian. This was particularly true of the maps published by the Soviet Union and some other countries who had not only used Iranian colours but also mentioned the Iranian names of the islands.[66]

Of the maps attributed to the Soviet Union in the above statement, a copy of one was given to this author by the Iranian Ministry of Foreign Affairs on 26 December 1971 and reproduced here as Fig. 9.3. In a recent interview with this author, Mr Amir Khosrow Afshar said:

> Representatives of Libya, South Yemen, Kuwait and Iraq addressed the meeting after my statement, each launched a strong attack against the Iranian regime, probably hoping for a reaction of similar kind from me, so that the hearing should continue and would come to a conclusion somewhat satisfactory for them. When I was asked to let the meeting know my reply I reaffirmed that I had not gone there to negotiate anything. I added that there was no power in the world that could make us leave these islands of ours, and that I had nothing else to add.

He continued:

> A silence followed my second statement and the representative of Somalia (a member of the Arab League) moved that the case should be let to rest. The motion was carried and the petition of complaint against Iran was shelved away.

Latest incidents

It was reported in April 1992 that Iranian authorities prevented entry into Abu Musa island of a group of Indian and Pakistani workers employed by the Emirate of Sharjah. The High Council of the United Arab Emirates met on 13 May to discuss "the issue" of Abu Musa island. It was reportedly agreed at the end of the meeting that the commitments of each member of the Union were to be treated as commitments of the Union as whole.[67] A representative of the United Arab Emirates visiting Tehran prior to this meeting, had suggested that a joint commission of representatives of Iran and the UAE should be formed to study the issue, but authorities of the Islamic Republic of Iran rejected the suggestion on the grounds that, first, there was no such thing as the issue of Abu Musa and, secondly, the agreement on Abu Musa was between Iran and Sharjah and no-one else had the right to interfere.[68]

Furthermore, it was reported on 24 August 1992 that Iranian authorities had prevented the entry into Abu Musa of more than 100 Arab teachers and their families who had gone there for a "pleasure trip".[69] Considering that Abu Musa is no more than a small desert island with a small village of 600 population and no significance of any kind save for its strategic importance for Iran, a pleasure trip of more than 100 teachers and their families from Sharjah without the prior knowledge of Iran would naturally be viewed in Tehran as a deliberate act designed to contravene its sovereignty over the whole of Abu Musa island.

Reporting the incident, *The Times* of London claimed that "Last month, Iran unilaterally reneged on that deal [of 1971], convincing many Western observers that it planned to use the island in the shipping lane which carried half of the world's oil as a base for three submarines that it is now purchasing from Russia".[70] The newspaper furthermore repeated claims made in Abu Dhabi and Cairo that Iran had asserted its full sovereignty over the whole of Abu Musa. Tehran denied all these claims and sent representatives to Abu Dhabi to find a peaceful end to the problem. These talks were brought to an abrupt end because the UAE asked for the two islands of Greater and Lesser Tunb to be ceded to them in addition to Abu Musa, a demand that left no doubt as to the true intentions of the UAE in the recent incident. The incident, however, was greeted by the UAE and some other Arab states, especially Egypt, with much anger. Shaikh Zaied Bin Sultan Al-Nahyan, president of the UAE, was reported to have noted in London in September 1992 that his government "was taking the dispute to international arbitration".[71] Iranian sources, meanwhile, made it clear that the reason for their action was that "in recent months suspicious activities were seen in the Arab part of Abu Musa Island"[72] that were aimed at undermining Iranian sovereignty of the island.

Reports from the military sources in Tehran say that without the permission of the Iranian Government, the United Arab Emirates were busy building new establishments in the non-military part of the island. It seems that with the agreement of certain Arab countries, a number of non-native Arabs are to become residents on the island in order to gradually put Iranian sovereignty of the island under doubt.[73]

Conclusion

The Iranian position on the ownership of the Persian Gulf islands of Abu Musa and the two Tunbs is currently under attack. Viewed from an Iranian standpoint, the reopening of the issue of the islands is unsettling and unacceptable. The claim of the United Arab Emirates to the three islands is regarded as unreasonable for the reasons given above. Perhaps the main objections in Iran arise from what is seen as the misuse of the historical record. The very recent emergence of the emirates as political and territorial units contrasts with the long history of Iranian dominance in the Persian Gulf region. The role of the Qasimi family at Lengeh, regarded as Iranian vassals, is not seen as conferring any rights on the contemporary Arab states of the region.

It is also clear that the obdurate nature of Iran's claims to the islands offers little optimism for a successful outcome to Arab counter-claims to ownership.

Notes

1. Abul-Hassan Ali ibn Hussein Masudi, *Moravvej az-Zahab*, 240, Persian translation (Tehran: Bongah-e Tarjomeh va Nashr-e Ketab, 1977).
2. Sir Arnold T. Wilson, *The Persian Gulf*, 55 (London: Allen & Unwin, 1928).
3. Ibid., 245–6.
4. Article 3 of the General Treaty for the Cessation of Plunder and Piracy by Land and Sea, 5 February 1820. Cited in D. Hawley, *The Trucial states*, 314 (London: Allen & Unwin, 1970).
5. J. G. Lorimer, *Gazetteer of the Persian Gulf, Oman and central Arabia*, vol. 1, 625 (Calcutta: Superintendent Government Printing Press, 1908).
6. J. B. Kelly, *Eastern Arabian frontiers*, 18 (London: Faber & Faber, 1964).
7. Lorimer , op. cit., 625.
8. Rev. G. P. Badger to the Government of Bombay. 5 June 1861 FO 60/385.
9. P. Mojtahed-Zadeh, *Shaikhneshinhay-ye Khalij-e Fars* [Shaikhdoms of the Persian Gulf] (Tehran: Ataei Publications, 1970).
10. J. C. Wilkinson, *Water and tribal settlement in southeast Arabia*, 8 (Oxford: Oxford University Press, 1977).
11. Including P. Mojtahed-Zadeh, *Political geography of the Strait of Hormuz*, 7–11 (London: SOAS, joint Department of Geography and Middle East Centre occasional paper, 1991).
12. Ibid., 8.
13. Ibid., 9.
14. Lorimer,op. cit., 1276.
15. Hawley, op. cit., 114.
16. K. Vadiei, *Joghrafiya-ye Ensani-e Iran* [Human geography of Iran], 192–3 (Tehran: Tehran University Press, no. 1280, 1974).
17. Lorimer, op. cit., 2086.
18. Ibid.

19. Hawley, op. cit., 162; the emirate of Ras al-Khaimah was separated from Sharjah and was so recognized by the British government in 1921.
20. Hawley, op. cit., 162.
21. Minute from the Customs Office of the Iranian Ministry of Finance to the Iranian Ministry of Foreign Affairs, 27 July 1927 (5 Mordad 1306).
22. Foreign Office confidential report (1961). FO 371/157031.
23. Minute by Mr Knatchbull-Hugessen to Mr A. Eden, Foreign Office, 9 April 1935. FO 371/18980 piece E2364/76/34. See also 1935 annual report for Tehran in FO 371/18980 piece E1147/1147/34.
24. Iranian Ministry of Foreign Affairs, Collection of Documents, Series 6300.
25. D. Wright, The English among the Persians, 66 (London: Heinemann, 1977).
26. Ibid., 67.
27. Ibid., 68.
28. Foreign Office confidential report (1961). FO 371/157031.
29. Ibid.
30. Ibid. Major P. Z. Cox to the Secretary of State to the Government of India, Foreign and Political Department, 12 June 1906.
31. FO 371/157031.
32. Ibid.
33. Extracted from confidential report of 8 January 1929 from Sir R. Clive to Sir A. Chamberlain. FO 371/157031.
34. Shaikh J. al-Eslami, Qatl-e Atabak, 213 (Tehran: Kayhan Publications, 1988).
35. Ibid.
36. Confidential report on visit of HMS Loch Insh to Tunb island by Captain R. M. Owen, 24 August 1961. FO 371/157031.
37. Ibid., 2.
38. Foreign Office to Political Resident in the Persian Gulf, 24 August 1961. FO 371/157031.
39. British Political Resident in the Persian Gulf to Foreign Office, 24 August 1961. FO 371/157031.
40. Note from British Embassy, Tehran, to Iranian Foreign Ministry, 5 September 1961. FO 371/157031.
41. Note from Iranian Foreign Ministry to British Embassy, Tehran, 21 September 1961. FO 371/157031.
42. Note from Foreign Office to G. E. Millard, British Embassy, Tehran, 2 November 1961. FO 371/157031.
43. Note from British Embassy, Tehran, to Iranian Foreign Ministry, 13 January 1962. FO 371/157031.
44. Al-Ahram, 10 November 1968.
45. Alam, Asadollah [ed. A. Alikhani], The Shah and I: the confidential diary of Iran's Royal Court, 1968–1977, 130 (London: I. B. Tauris, 1991).
46. Hawley, op. cit., 287–8.
47. Kayhan International, 30 May 1970.
48. Mohammad Reza Shah in an interview with Associated Press, Kayhan International, 5 June 1971.
49. Kayhan International, 27 June 1971.
50. Amir Abbas Hovaida in Bandar Abbas, Ettela'at Havai'i, 27 June 1971.
51. Comments from the Shaikh of Sharjah, Al-Ahram (Cairo), 8 December 1971; see also, R. N. Schofield's contribution to round-table discussion on the disputed Gulf islands, Arab Research Centre, London, 18 November 1992.
52. Mojtahed-Zadeh, op. cit., 21.
53. A. Cottrell, Iran: diplomacy in a regional and global context, The Washington Papers 6 (Los Angeles: Sage, 1974).

54. R. K. Ramazani, *The Persian Gulf: Iran's role*, 56–8. (Charlottesville: University Press of Virginia, 1972).

55. *Al-Ahram* (Cairo), 8 December 1971.

56. *Kayhan International*, 30 November 1971.

57. United Nations, *Monthly chronicle: record of the month of December 1971*, **9**(1), 46 (1972, New York).

58. Ibid.

59. Ibid.

60. Ibid., 59.

61. Ibid., 47.

62. *Kayhan International*, 8 October 1992.

63. United Nations, op. cit., 48.

64. Ibid.

65. Amir Khosrow Afshar was then Iran's ambassador to the United Kingdom. He became locum minister for foreign affairs and was one of the last foreign ministers under the monarchical regime.

66. *Iran Almanac*, 265 (Tehran: Echo Publications, 1972).

67. *Echo of Iran*, 9 (London: Echo Publications, May 1992).

68. Ibid.

69. BBC, *Persian Service News Bulletin*, 25 August 1992.

70. *The Times*, 11 (London), 22 September 1992.

71. Ibid.

72. *Echo of Iran* (1992), 3.

73. Ibid., 4.

CHAPTER TEN
The eastern boundaries of Iran

PIROUZ MOJTAHED-ZADEH

Introduction

The eastern boundaries of Iran are the geographical manifestation of a long political process of two powers – Iran and Britain – acting in rivalry against each other. Historically, Iran's eastern frontiers had, until the mid–19th century, never had a clearly defined geographical limit. These frontiers, depending on the strength and weakness of the central authorities in Iran, moved back and forth across central Asia. They sometimes included places as far east as Kabul and what is now northern India, while such places as Bokhara, Samarqand, Merv, Khivah, Balkh and Herat featured prominently in Persian literature as traditional Iranian cities.

These fluctuations in Iran's eastern territorial limits were much more pronounced in the post-Islamic era, each dynasty ruling within a territorial limit greatly differing from that of the others.

With the rise of the Safavid empire (1501–1722), Iran recovered most of its pre-Islamic territories, extending its geographical limits to match those of the Sassanids. In the east, the Safavids successfully established Iranian sovereignty over central Asia, yet geographical and political centres such as Kabul and Herat maintained some degree of autonomy within the empire.

Safavid rule was brought to an end by a rebellion of Afghan tribes in central Asia, which raided the capital Isfahan, not as outsiders, but as revolutionaries from within. Their rebellion was put down by Nadir Qoli Afshar, whose rule not only revived Iran's traditional realms in the east, but also pushed its influence well within the Indian subcontinent.

Nadir Shah's assassination in June 1747 coincided with the rise to prominence of the British Indian empire, the rivalries between which and other European powers, particularly the Russians, triggered the process of disintegration of the Iranian authority in central Asia.

128

Figure 10.1 The eastern boundaries of Iran.

The partitioning of Khorasan, Sistan and Baluchistan

Following Nadir Shah's assassination, the Afghan and Uzbak contingents of the Naderi forces, commanded by Nur Mohammad Khan and Ahmad Khan Abdali, began their fateful march towards Qandahar, where they decided to use the opportune moment of a leaderless Iran to establish their own kingdoms. Thus, Ahmad Khan Abdali was selected as leader and was given the title Shah of Afghanistan. Amir Alam Khan I Khozeimeh, another able general of the Naderi forces and ruler of the Khozeimeh amirdom of Qaenat, conquered Mashad and Herat, the two principal governorates of Khorasan. This military undertaking expanded the Khozeimeh amirdom to include Khorasan, Sistan and Baluchistan. News of his conquests diverted Ahmad Shah Abdali's attention from India to Khorasan. Herat fell after a stiff resistance and the eastern half of Khorasan was occupied. Amir Alam Khan was preparing for a second expedition when he was murdered by his own father-in-law in 1749.[1]

By the turn of the 19th century, Herat was returned to Iran in the form of an autonomous governorate. As from 1810, a series of revolts began in Herat by the Iranian governor of the province. When Kameran Khan styled himself in 1829 as the Shah of Herat and began to interfere in the affairs of Sistan, the Qajar Shah of Iran moved troops to Herat where they began the siege of the city in 1837.

Kameran, deprived of assistance from Dust Mohammad Khan of Kabul, who declined to interfere "in the internal affairs of Iran", turned to Sir John McNeil, British Minister at Tehran, for assistance. McNeil left Tehran in the spring 1838, suspending Anglo–Iranian relations. In a petition to Lord Palmerston he advised the British Government to intervene in Afghanistan, since "the fall of Herat would destroy our position in Afghanistan, and place all, or nearly all, that country under the influence or authority of Russia and Persia".[2] Acting upon McNeil's suggestion, the British government in India despatched a naval task force from Bombay, which occupied the Iranian island of Kharg. This action, together with Kameran Khan's renewed declaration of loyalty to Tehran, averted the fall of Herat.

On 15 September 1855, the Iranian governor of Herat was murdered by his deputy, Nayeb Isa Khan, who moved troops towards Sistan. The rebellion was seen in Tehran as a serious threat to Sistan. On the decision of Prime Minister Mirza Agha Khan Sadr Azam Nouri, Iranian troops seized Herat in April 1856 and occupied the city. In November of that year, Britain declared war on Iran and a number of Iranian ports and islands were occupied by British forces in the Persian Gulf.

The Qajar Shah was forced to accept peace at the Paris treaty of March 1857. Article 6 of this treaty paved the way for the official separation of Herat and the final partition of Khorasan. The first paragraph of this article read: "His Majesty the Shah of Persia agrees to relinquish all claims to sov-

ereignty over the territory and city of Herat and the countries of Afghanistan . . ."[3] Furthermore, the Treaty of Paris prepared the ground for the
emergence of Iran's eastern boundaries. The last paragraph of Article 6 also
provided:

> In case of differences arising between the Government of Persia and
> the countries of Herat and Afghanistan, the Persian Government en-
> gages to refer them for adjustment to the friendly offices of the British
> Government and not to take up arms unless those friendly offices fail
> of effect.[4]

Following these developments, Herat was declared an independent principality and remained so until 1862, when Dust Mohammad Khan Amir of
Kabul moved into Qandahar and Herat and began interfering in Sistan
affairs. The Iranian government complained to the British in 1863 and requested arbitration in accordance with Article 6 of the 1857 treaty. In response, Foreign Secretary Lord Russell sent a letter to Tehran in November
1863 stating:

> Her Majesty's Government, being informed that the title of territory
> of Sistan is disputed between Persia and Afghanistan, must decline to
> interfere in this matter, and leave it to both parties to make good their
> possessions by force of arms.[5]

Upon receiving this letter, Amir Alam Khan III Khozeimeh's forces moved to
the east of the Hirmand delta and successfully recovered the occupied half of
Sistan. The Kabul government complained to the British Government of India
and the Iranian government to London, each demanding arbitration.

Goldsmid and the partitioning of Baluchistan

Baluchistan district – from the River Hirmand to the coasts of the Indian
ocean, and from the Indus to Kirman – was under Iranian sovereignty
throughout the Safavid era. The rise to power of Nadir Shah in 1737 guar-
anteed Baluchistan's return to Iranian sovereignty after a brief period of confusion. Several tribal chiefs claimed independence following Nadir Shah's
assassination in June 1747. As Ahmad Shah Abdali's appointed governor of
Kalat, Nasir Khan, claimed independence following his master's death in
1773, the westwardly expanding interests of British India provided him with
its support against Iranian pressure. On the death of Nasir Khan in 1795,
Baluchistan was divided among local chieftains, some of whom accepted
British protection while others remained loyal to Iran. This development
divided the province into British-protected Baluchistan (Kalat) and Iranian
Baluchistan.

Claim of sovereignty to the whole of Baluchistan was revived by Mohammad Shah Qajar (1834–47) and Bampur was taken from rebellious chiefs in

1849. The newly appointed governor of Kirman, Ibrahim Khan, subsequently recovered Geh, Qasrequand and Sarbaz. Isfandak and Chah Bahar were recovered in 1872. Chah Bahar had hitherto been held by the Arabs of Muscat, administering the port and the district on behalf of the Iranian government in accordance with an agreement between the two parties.[6] Bashagard was recovered in 1874. Among other chiefs, the Khan of Kalat remained independent of Iran as a result of protection provided to him by the British, while those of less power attempted to maintain their semi-independent status.

This chaotic situation caused friction between Iran and the Britain, which needed a well defined boundary in order to extend its telegraph line westward from Gwadur to Jask and the Strait of Hormuz.

In 1870, however, it was agreed to settle the dispute by arbitration and a commission was formed to fix the boundary. In 1871, Sir Frederic Goldsmid and Mirza Masum Khan Ansari were assigned to the task and began their work. The lack of trust between the two commissioners led to much delay[7] and it was possible only to define, but not demarcate, the frontier from Gwadur Bay, on the Indian ocean, as far as Jalq. It soon proved impossible to reach agreement over the town of Kuhak on the Mashkil river, and this question was left to be settled later. Immediately after the departure of Goldsmid in 1872, Ibrahim Khan recovered Kuhak and some other parts of the Mashkil valley. This action, together with increasing disputes between some Iranian tribes and the Nushirvanis of Kharan, led to renewed frictions between Iran and British India, which necessitated another move for the settlement of the border dispute.

A second boundary commission was appointed in 1895 to define and demarcate the entire frontier from the coast to the Kuh-e Malek Siyah where the Iranian/Afghan/Kalat (now Pakistan) boundaries met. Tension arose between the two commissioners that prevented agreement on a number of points. Although the frontier was defined, demarcation was carried out on only a short length of the boundary:

> demarcation was carried out only from the Mashkil river, 6½ miles east by south of Kuhak to the southern edge of the Hamun-i-Mashkel and thence in a west-south-westerly direction for 11 miles to the right bank of the Talah river, a total distance of 126¼ miles.[8]

The agreement relating to the demarcation of the boundary between the two countries, signed at Jalq on 24 March 1896, recognized Kuhak's status as an Iranian possession. The agreement described the boundary thus:

> From pillar 11 northwards to the Talah river becomes the boundary to its junction with the Mirjawa river. From the point of junction it is carried by a straight line to the nearest point on the watershed of the Mirjawa range, which limits the drainage into the Mirjawa river on the north. Thence it follows the main watershed northwards to the highest point of the Kach Koh. From the highest point of the Kacha Koh

the line is carried straight to the highest point of Malek Siah Koh.[9]

The Iranians did not send a commissioner to survey the above-mentioned frontier areas, and Holdich (the British commissioner) continued the work unilaterally. The result was that the boundary was not marked on the ground but simply described and marked on existing maps, which proved to be inaccurate. Friction occurred between the two parties, especially with respect to the status of Mirjawah. In an exchange of notes in 1902, both parties agreed to appoint another arbitration commission, but the British agreed on 13 March 1905 to recognize Mirjawah as belonging to Iran in exchange for concessions in Sistan, where Amir Ali-Akbar Khan Khozeimeh's imminent dismissal from the hereditary governorship was viewed by Britain as a loss of face in front of Russian rivals. The 1896 agreement and the 1905 British concession in respect of Mirjawah left two portions of these boundaries undemarcated: first, the stretch from Gwadur Bay to the Mashkil river and, secondly, the stretch from southwest of Hamun-e Mashkil to the Kuh-e Malek Siyah. In spite of the fact that the newly created state of Pakistan continued negotiations with Iran on these disputed area, parts of their common borders still remain to be demarcated in full and final settlement.

Goldsmid arbitration and the partitioning of Sistan

As the governments of both Iran and Kabul complained to the British, requesting arbitration, Sir Frederic Goldsmid was assigned in 1870 to lead the Sistan arbitration. He spent the year 1871 defining the frontier between Iran and what was then British Baluchistan (now Pakistan) and the following year surveying border areas in Sistan. Highly suspicious of British designs, Amir Alam Khan III Khozeimeh created problems in the task of arbitration. Amir Alam Khan demonstrated his power and influence to such an extent that he convinced Britain that it would be inadvisable to deprive Iran of the whole of Sistan. Reporting to the government in British India, Goldsmid asserted: "Ameer of Kain has great power. [The] Persian commissioner plays his game and talks of Lord Russell's despatch, arguing that no present possession is to be discussed."[10] Based on this information, London asked General Pollock, Adviser to the Afghan commissioner, who was not permitted by Amir Alam Khan to enter Sistan, the following:

> Persia holds chief part of Sistan so firmly that arbitral opinion must be in favour of Persia, but . . . would such a boundary [the River Hirmand], though not giving all that is desired, satisfy sufficiently Afghan interests . . . ?[11]

The Khozeimeh Amir of Qaenat and Sistan therefore influenced the boundary arbitration greatly, as did his predecessors before him. The role of the Khozeimeh family is little known in Iran.

The arbitration commission, however, resolved that Sistan should be partitioned into outer and inner sections, giving Iran inner Sistan and Afghanistan outer Sistan, defining the main branch of the River Hirmand as the boundary between the two countries. The basis for this decision was argued to have been historical and actual possessions in the region. Iran accepted the outcome with reluctance and Amir Alam Khan was instructed by Tehran to surrender his amirdom's possessions, private lands and villages to the east of the River Hirmand to Afghanistan.

The MacLean arbitration of the Khorasan boundaries

The Khorasan boundaries, which are the northern sector of Iran's eastern frontiers, are 819 kilometres, starting from the Zulfiqar pass to the north and ending at Malek Siyah Kuh in the south. This section of the frontier was largely delimited after Goldsmid's arbitration work was completed. The boundaries are the result of at least three arbitrations, the first of which was that of Major-General MacLean in 1888. This arbitration was prompted by a dispute between Iran and Afghanistan in the Hashtadan region. MacLean was assigned to arbitrate, survey and define the frontier from the Hashtadan plain, some 100 kilometres to the west of the city of Herat, to the Zulfiqar pass, where the Iran/Afghan/Russian frontiers met. This stretch was demarcated by MacLean in July 1891.

The boundary line measures 103 miles and consists of 39 turning points. Mozaffar ed-Din Shah accepted it only on condition that the "the Hashtadan hill (under two acres) is included in Iranian territory and the word (Hashtadan) is marked on the Iranian side of the map".[12] MacLean succeeded in obtaining this concession after interviewing Mozaffar ed-Din Shah in Brighton during his visit in July 1889, when MacLean found the Qajar Shah totally ignorant of the nature of the Hashtadan dispute.[13] The following is a brief description of the frontier as it appears on the map attached to a Foreign Office memorandum:

> The line commences at the northern point of the kuh-i-Kadanna passes round the heads of the southern group of Kanats, so as to include these in Afghan territory, and up to the head of the short Kanat immediately north of the Hashtadan mound, leaving the mound on the Persian side of the line. Thence across to the foot of the hills, and thence due north to the crest of the Sanjitti range. The line then follows the crest of the range eastward to the crest of the hills on the northern side of the Dhana-i-Shoraab, and thence in a straight line to a point on the left bank of the Kal-i-Kala 300 yards below the place where the old canal takes off towards Kafir Kala – the line then follows the Kal-i-Kala up to the Hari-Rud.[14]

The McMahon arbitration of the Sistan boundaries

Following Goldsmid's Sistan arbitration of 1872, further disputes occurred between Iran and Afghanistan on the Sistan boundaries. In 1896, the river changed course and British arbitration was requested. Colonel McMahon was assigned to lead the arbitration. He spent several years in the region and by 1903 determined that the boundary should be placed on the old river channel. His arbitration followed the same pattern as Goldsmid's except that he allocated two-thirds of the Hirmand waters to the Afghan side of Sistan, which is barren, and one-third to Iranian Sistan, which is fertile and populous. Demarcation of the Sistan boundary was completed in 1905.

The portion of the frontier settled by arbitration began at the Kuh-e Malek Siyah, whence it ran northeastwards for 130 kilometres to the Hirmand; it then turned northwards, leaving Nastratabad (Zabol) in Iran, and Chakhansur in Afghanistan. Forty-eight kilometres north-northeast of Zabol the frontier swung round almost due west and ran for 106 kilometres across the northern section of Lake Hamun, to a point just to the east of the peak known as the Siyah Kuh, making a total of 277 kilometres.

The Altai arbitration and the Qaenat boundaries

By the 1930s, 165 kilometres of the boundary line in the northern section was delimited and demarcated by the MacLean arbitration and 277 kilometres of the middle section was delimited and demarcated by the McMahon arbitration. Yet the 377 kilometres between these two sectors remained unsettled, primarily between the Qaenat district and Afghanistan.

From 1930 onwards, a number of disputes and minor clashes occurred over Musa-Abad, a hamlet in the Hashtadan district close to the northern end of the unsettled frontier, and the district of Yazdan, where the Khozeimeh amirs of Qaenat and Sistan had reconstructed the old qanats and developed a few irrigation systems for small patches of cultivable lands.

Both Iran and Afghanistan decided to go to arbitration. This time, the Turks were asked to arbitrate these disputed frontier areas. General Fakhred-Din Altai, having examined the claims of the two parties, defined and demarcated the 377 kilometres between the MacLean and McMahon sections. The boundary, demarcated in 1935, left the hamlet and springs of Musa-Abad to Iran, while Afghanistan received the winter pastures (Qeshlaq) to the east of Musa-Abad where certain Afghan tribes assembled.[15]

The Yazdan district had traditionally belonged to the Khozeimeh family of Qaenat and Sistan and it was in possession of Amir Mohammad Reza Khan Khozeimeh at the time of arbitration. Afghanistan claimed the district on the basis that ancestors of the local Afghan tribesmen had been buried there. As the investigation continued, it became apparent that the Afghans buried in Yazdan had been slain and buried by Khozeimeh armed forces while being chased out of Qaenat after having carried out a raid on that district.

An old qanat, revived in Yazdan at the turn of the 20th century, was left on the Iranian side of the boundary, while the source of the qanat, together with patches of agricultural lands and orchards belonging to the Khozeimeh Amir, were given to Afghanistan. To the southwest of the Yazdan district there existed another qanat, which had been revitalized by Amir Hussain Khan Khozeimeh, and the district around it, as far as Kabudeh, was irrigated and named Taher-Abad (after the Amir's daughter Tahereh). Here, too, the qanat and its immediate vicinity were assigned to Iran; the well's source and lands to the east of the qanat were given to Afghanistan. The Namakzar (salt lake), with salt deposits of some value, which was disputed between the two countries, was divided equally between them by a line running from north to south. Both Iran and Afghanistan accepted Altai's awards and the demarcation of the entire frontier between the two countries was completed in the same year.[16]

The Hirmand water agreement of 1939

From 1929 onwards, disputes over the use of water from the Hirmand river continued between Iran and Afghanistan, mainly because the latter had tried to draw more water from the river than the two-thirds allocated to it by the McMahon arbitration of 1903.

In 1931, it was reported that the Afghans had begun clearing the bed of the old Shahi canal, above Band Sistan, which, if used, would deprive Iranian Sistan of water.[17] The dispute continued after the Altai arbitration was completed, and direct negotiations between the two countries resulted in the signing of the 1939 treaty whereby the boundary was to follow the centre of the stream and the water was to be divided equally between the two countries.[18] Article 1 of the treaty reads: "The two powers will divide the water of the Hirmand, throughout the year, in equal portions, from the Band Kamal Khan."[19] This agreement, though a significant improvement from the Iranian point of view, failed to put an end to the border dispute. Afghanistan, with the help of the United States, constructed a number of dams and canals, diverting more than half of the Hirmand waters before they reached Iran's borders, thus depriving a highly fertile and populous region of this important natural resource.

The dispute continued in the Hirmand delta, and even the Sadabad Pact[20] of 1937 – giving implicit recognition to existing boundary arrangements in the region – did not put an end to the differences. The Afghans continued diverting more water from the Hirmand before it reached Band Kamal Khan, further aggravating the problem of poor water supply from the Hirman river.

In 1945, Afghanistan signed a series of agreements with American companies for the construction of dams and canals on the River Hirmand. Within eight years, between 1949–57, the Abgardan (diversion) Boghra dam was constructed at Girishk and the 70 km Boghra canal was built with a capacity of 1.5 million ft³. The Arghandab dam was constructed on the Arghandab branch of the Hirmand river. Also, the Hoghian, Kamareq, Akhtechi, Gohargan, Juy-e No, Archi Sarvi and a number of other canals were constructed in Afghanistan with disastrous effects on Iranian Sistan. This area, frequently referred to in historical documents as the "bread basket" of Khorasan, which owed much of its economic life to the free flow of the Hirmand river and Lake Hamun or Sistan lake, is now almost a desert.

At the turn of the 20th century, G. P. Tate described the catchment area of Sistan lake as covering something like 240,000 square kilometres, its length from northeast to southwest being 950 kilometres and its greatest width being 560 kilometres.[21] Colonel Yate, also writing on the geographical features around Sistan lake at the turn of the century, described the Neyzar or reed forest as being several kilometres thick on the eastern side of the lake alone.[22]

Lake Hamun has gradually disappeared and with it has gone almost the whole of the Neyzar. The Hamun was not only the main source of irrigation in the central and western parts of Sistan, but also provided many water-associated economic activities such as fishing, hunting in the Neyzar, grazing pastures for livestock, the ferrying of goods and passengers across the lake. The Neyzar created many opportunities in handicraft industries for the inhabitants. With the disappearance of the main body of the lake and the Neyzar, all of these economic activities disappeared, while the damage to agriculture has forced many inhabitants to migrate from Sistan. The flooding of the Hirmand river in recent years – which has revived Lake Hamun temporarily – does not represent a change of policy in Afghanistan but illustrates the lack of control of the river, both politically and technically.

Conclusion

The governments and peoples of Iran have learned to accept and be content with the country's international boundaries, largely consolidated during the 20th century. It must be a matter of some regret, however, that valuable territories have been lost through the incompetence and ignorance of those who ruled the country at the time the borders were delimited. The efforts of local rulers such as Khozeimeh of Qaenat and Sistan to protect Iranian interests were generally beneficial. The concerns of the Khozeimeh family with farming and irrigation gave them the local knowledge and economic incentive to fight for a maximal portion of both territory and above all water supply. In so far as these local families' interests coincided closely with national policies, Iran benefited from the activities of its regional elite. When local advice, *inter alia* from the Alam or Khozeimeh families, was ignored by the Iranian central authorities, national interests were also badly served, as is illustrated by the continuing border problems faced in the Sistan basin and adjacent territories.

A factor strongly affecting boundaries in eastern Iran is the way in which the international border divides people of the same ethnic origin and shared historic roots. At the same time, uncertainty over the full and final settlement of the border, as is the case in central Sistan, engenders insecurity among the rural populations and has led to the abandonment of erstwhile fertile lands.

Iran–Afghanistan relations have been much damaged by disputes over the Hirmand river and its tributaries, and general co-operation will not be possible until the causes for these border areas are justly settled.

Notes

1. P. Mojtahed-Zadeh, "Bar Sistan va Hirmand che gozshteh ast", *Rahavard* **25** (Winter 1990), 262–71.
2. Sir John McNeil to Viscount Palmerston, 11 April 1838. FO 539/1-10.
3. Article 6, Paris Treaty, 2 March 1857. FO 60/403.
4. Ibid.
5. A. Bilgrami, *Afghanistan and British India*, 145 (New Delhi: Sterling Publishers, 1972).
6. Rev. G. P. Badger to the Government of Bombay, 5 June 1861. FO 60/385.
7. For more details, see Mojtahed-Zadeh, op. cit.
8. Foreign Office memorandum, "Persia's frontiers with Baluchistan", 11. E101361/4029/34 in FO 371/45507.
9. Ibid.
10. Goldsmid to Foreign Secretary, Calcutta, 12 April 1872. FO 60/392.
11. Foreign Secretary, Calcutta, to General Pollock, 27 April 1872. FO 60/392.
12. Telegram from British Minister at Tehran to Viceroy of India, 7 December 1889. FO 60/538.
13. Notes of MacLean's interview with Shah at Brighton. FO 60/538.
14. Memorandum, undated. FO 60/538.
15. British Legation, Tehran, to Foreign Office, 10 January 1935. FO 371/19408.
16. British Legation, Tehran, to Foreign Office, 22 May 1935. FO 371/19408.
17. Telegram from Government of India to Secretary of State of Foreign Affairs, London, 16 November 1931. FO 371/15550.
18. British Legation, Tehran, to Foreign Office, 14 November 1935. FO 371/19408.
19. Translation of French text, *Journal de Téhéran*. FO 371/23264.

NOTES

20. Both Iran and Afghanistan, together with Pakistan, Turkey and Iraq, were signatories to the Sadabad pact.
21. G. P. Tate, *The frontiers of Baluchistan*, 237 (London: Witherby, 1909).
22. Lt. Col. C. E. Yate, *Khorasan and Sistan*, 81 (Edinburgh & London: William Blackwood, 1900).

Index